Tariffs:

A Double Edged Sword

Tariffs: A Double Edged Sword

History, Impact, and the
Future
of Protectionism in the U.S. Economy

Francis Williams

ISBN: 978-1-0693414-0-2

Tariffs: A Double-Edged Sword - History, Impact, and the Future of Protectionism in the U.S. Economy

"The philosophy of protectionism is a philosophy of war."

~ Ludwig von Mises

"Trade wars are good and easy to win."

~ Donald Trump (2018)

Trade barriers may protect the present, but free and fair commerce builds the future."

~ Anonymous

To the new leaders of the fourth turning.

Disclaimer

This book is intended for informational and educational purposes only. While every effort has been made to ensure the accuracy of the content, the author and publisher make no representations or warranties regarding the completeness, reliability, or suitability of the information provided.

The economic and trade policies discussed in this book are subject to change, and their effects may vary based on geopolitical events, market conditions, and policy decisions. Readers are encouraged to consult official government sources, trade experts, and financial professionals before making decisions related to tariffs, trade policies, or economic strategies.

This book does not provide financial, legal, or investment advice. The views expressed are those of the author and do not necessarily reflect the positions of any government, organization, or institution. The author and publisher disclaim any liability for errors, omissions, or outcomes resulting from the use of this book.

All trade agreements, policies, and historical references mentioned are for discussion and analysis only. Any trademarks, product names, or government documents referenced remain the property of their respective owners.

By reading this book, you agree that the author and publisher shall not be held responsible for any economic, financial, or policy-related decisions made based on the content presented.

Note to the Reader

This book was created with the assistance of AI-powered tools, which were used to research, format, organize, and edit the material presented. Artificial intelligence helped streamline the writing process by structuring historical data, analyzing economic theories, and synthesizing complex trade policies into a clear and readable format.

While AI played a significant role in compiling and refining the content, human oversight was essential in ensuring accuracy, coherence, and contextual relevance. The material was reviewed, fact-checked, and edited to maintain a high standard of quality and objectivity.

As with any book on economics and policy, readers are encouraged to continue researching, questioning, and engaging with experts to develop their own informed perspectives on the role of tariffs in global trade. AI-assisted content creation is an evolving field, and its application in research and writing represents an exciting step toward making complex topics more accessible.

Thank you for reading, and we hope this book provides valuable insights into the history, impact, and future of tariffs in the U.S. and beyond.

Tariffs: A Double-Edged Sword
History, Impact, and the
Future
of Protectionism in the U.S. Economy

Table of Contents

Part 3: Tariffs in Today's Economic Environment

Part 4: Evaluating Tariffs for the Future

Introduction

Few economic policies spark as much debate as tariffs. Are they shields that protect industries or weapons that ignite trade wars? They have been praised as shields that protect domestic industries and workers, but they have also been condemned as economic weapons that increase prices, stifle competition, and provoke trade wars. The question of whether tariffs are beneficial or harmful is far from simple—it depends on the context, the implementation, and the broader economic environment in which they are used.

In today's interconnected world, where supply chains stretch across multiple countries and global trade drives economic growth, tariffs remain a contentious issue. The United States has oscillated between protectionism and free trade for over two centuries, with each shift influenced by economic crises, political ideologies, and evolving global dynamics. While some see tariffs as a necessary tool to protect American jobs and industries, others warn that they may do more harm than good by increasing costs and reducing international cooperation.

This book takes a deep dive into the complex world of tariffs, exploring their history, economic impact, and the differing perspectives on their use. It will examine when and where tariffs have succeeded, when they have failed, and what lessons the U.S. can learn from past experiences. With trade policy being a key factor in today's economic debates—especially in light of tensions with China, the restructuring of NAFTA into the USMCA, and the growing demand for domestic manufacturing—understanding tariffs is more critical than ever.

Why This Book Matters Now

As the U.S. grapples with challenges such as global supply chain disruptions, inflation, and geopolitical tensions, trade policy is once again at the forefront of economic discussions. Policymakers are debating whether tariffs can help rebuild domestic industries, counter China's economic influence, or protect national security interests. At the same time, businesses and consumers are feeling the effects of increased costs and trade uncertainty.

This book aims to provide a balanced and nuanced perspective on tariffs, analyzing both historical and modern case studies to evaluate their effectiveness. Instead of taking a one-sided approach, it will present the economic, political, and practical realities of tariffs, helping readers understand their potential benefits and risks.

In the chapters ahead, we will explore:

- The economic theories behind tariffs
- Historical examples of tariffs that succeeded or failed
- The modern global trade environment and the role tariffs play today
- Who benefits from tariffs and who bears the cost
- Policy recommendations for the U.S. moving forward

By the end of this book, readers will have a clear understanding of how tariffs shape economies, why they remain controversial, and what the future may hold for U.S. trade policy. Whether you are a policymaker, business owner, economist, or simply someone interested in global trade, this book will equip you with the knowledge to critically evaluate tariffs and their impact on the modern world.

Now, let's begin by exploring the fundamentals of tariffs, their economic implications, and the historical context that has shaped their role in trade policy.

Chapter 1: What Are Tariffs?

Tariffs are one of the oldest and most widely used tools in economic policy. They serve as a mechanism for regulating trade between nations, protecting domestic industries, and generating government revenue. However, their impact varies depending on how they are applied, the economic environment in which they function, and the reactions of other countries.

In this chapter, we will define tariffs in detail, explore their different types, and examine how they function within the global economy. We will also discuss why governments impose tariffs and how they influence businesses, consumers, and trade relations.

1.1 Defining Tariffs

At its core, a tariff is a tax or duty imposed on imported goods. When a government places a tariff on a product, it increases the cost of that imported item, making it more expensive than similar domestically produced goods. The primary goal of a tariff is to either protect local industries from foreign competition or generate revenue for the government.

For example, if the U.S. imposes a 10% tariff on imported steel, a foreign steel producer must pay an additional 10% tax on the price of the steel they sell to American buyers. This makes imported steel more expensive and gives American steel producers a competitive advantage.

Tariffs can be applied to a wide range of goods, from raw materials like aluminum and oil to finished products like cars, electronics, and clothing.

1.2 Types of Tariffs

There are several types of tariffs, each serving a different purpose in economic and trade policy.

1.2.1 Ad Valorem Tariffs

These tariffs are calculated as a percentage of the value of the imported good.

- **Example:** A 15% tariff on imported televisions means that if a television costs $500, an additional $75 tariff is added, making the total cost $575.

1.2.2 Specific Tariffs

These tariffs are fixed fees imposed per unit of an imported good, regardless of its price.

- **Example:** A tariff of $5 per pair of imported shoes means that no matter the price of the shoes, an importer must pay $5 extra per pair.

1.2.3 Compound Tariffs

These tariffs combine elements of both ad valorem and specific tariffs.

- **Example:** A 10% ad valorem tariff + $3 per unit on imported smartphones means an importer must pay both a percentage of the phone's value and a fixed fee per unit.

1.2.4 Revenue Tariffs

These tariffs are primarily designed to raise government revenue rather than to protect local industries.

- **Example:** A country with a weak tax collection system might impose tariffs on foreign goods as a way to generate income.

1.2.5 Protective Tariffs

These tariffs are intended to protect domestic industries by making foreign goods more expensive.

- **Example:** If the U.S. imposes a 30% tariff on foreign cars, American consumers are more likely to buy cars produced domestically.

1.2.6 Retaliatory Tariffs

These tariffs are used as a response to another country's trade policies and are often imposed as part of a trade war.

- **Example:** If the U.S. places tariffs on Chinese steel, China may retaliate by imposing tariffs on American agricultural products.

1.2.7 Import vs. Export Tariffs

- Import Tariffs are taxes placed on goods coming into a country (most common type).

- Export Tariffs are taxes placed on goods leaving a country (less common, but sometimes used to control the supply of certain goods, such as oil or rare minerals).

1.3 How Tariffs Work

When a tariff is imposed, it increases the price of imported goods in the domestic market. The immediate effects of tariffs include:

- Higher prices for consumers – Since tariffs add to the cost of imports, businesses often pass these costs onto consumers in the form of higher prices.

- Reduced competition – Domestic industries benefit because foreign competitors face additional costs, making local goods relatively cheaper.

- Increased government revenue – Governments collect money from tariffs, which can be used for public services or infrastructure.

However, the long-term effects of tariffs can be complex, as they often provoke retaliation from other countries, potentially leading to reduced exports and economic inefficiencies.

1.4 Why Governments Impose Tariffs

Governments impose tariffs for several reasons, including:

1.4.1 Protecting Domestic Industries

Tariffs protect local businesses by making foreign products more expensive, reducing competition. This is especially important in industries where countries want to develop self-sufficiency, such as manufacturing, agriculture, and defense.

- **Example**: The U.S. imposed tariffs on foreign solar panels to support American solar panel manufacturers.

1.4.2 Reducing Trade Deficits

A trade deficit occurs when a country imports more than it exports. Tariffs can help reduce imports, theoretically improving a country's trade balance.

- **Example:** The U.S. has a significant trade deficit with China, leading to the use of tariffs to discourage reliance on Chinese goods.

1.4.3 Retaliation Against Unfair Trade Practices

Tariffs can be used as a tool to counteract perceived unfair trade practices, such as dumping (selling goods below cost to drive competitors out of business) or currency manipulation.

- **Example:** The European Union imposed tariffs on Chinese electric vehicles after accusations of unfair government subsidies.

1.4.4 Generating Government Revenue

In some cases, tariffs are a primary source of government funding, especially in countries with weak tax collection systems.

- **Example:** In the 19th century, before income taxes existed, the U.S. relied heavily on tariff revenue to fund the government.

1.4.5 National Security Concerns

Governments sometimes impose tariffs to protect industries deemed critical for national security.

- **Example:** The U.S. imposed tariffs on imported steel and aluminum, arguing that domestic production is essential for military and infrastructure needs.

1.5 The Global Impact of Tariffs

In today's interconnected world, tariffs do not exist in isolation. When one country imposes tariffs, it often leads to countermeasures by other nations, sometimes escalating into full-blown trade wars.

- **Example:** The U.S.-China Trade War (2018-2020)

  - The U.S. imposed tariffs on $250 billion worth of Chinese goods.

  - China retaliated with tariffs on American soybeans, cars, and other exports.

  - Both countries suffered economic losses as businesses scrambled to adjust.

Tariffs also influence global supply chains, as companies shift production to countries with lower tariff rates. For example, when tariffs were placed on Chinese goods, many companies moved production to Vietnam and Mexico to avoid the extra costs.

Conclusion

Tariffs are a powerful but controversial economic tool. While they can protect domestic industries, generate revenue, and correct trade imbalances, they also raise prices for consumers and risk provoking retaliatory measures.

Understanding the different types of tariffs and their impact on trade is essential for evaluating their effectiveness. In the next chapter, we will dive deeper into the economic theories behind tariffs, examining how they fit into the broader debate between protectionism and free trade.

Chapter 2: The Economic Theories Behind Tariffs

Tariffs have been a part of economic policy for centuries, but economists remain deeply divided on their effectiveness. Some argue that tariffs are necessary to protect domestic industries, support economic independence, and strengthen national security. Others warn that tariffs create inefficiencies, increase costs for consumers, and stifle economic growth.

This chapter explores the major economic theories behind tariffs, from classical arguments for free trade to modern justifications for protectionism. By understanding these theories, we can better evaluate when tariffs might be beneficial and when they might be harmful.

2.1 Free Trade vs. Protectionism

The debate over tariffs is part of a larger economic discussion between free trade and protectionism.

- Free trade promotes the unrestricted exchange of goods and services across borders, allowing countries to specialize in industries where they have a competitive advantage.

- Protectionism advocates for tariffs, quotas, and other trade barriers to shield domestic industries from foreign competition.

Both approaches have advantages and disadvantages, and different countries have applied them in various ways throughout history.

2.2 Classical Free Trade Theories

The foundation of modern free trade theory was laid by Adam Smith and David Ricardo in the late 18th and early 19th centuries.

2.2.1 Adam Smith and Absolute Advantage

In his book The Wealth of Nations (1776), Adam Smith argued against tariffs and trade restrictions. He introduced the concept of absolute advantage, which states that:

"A country should specialize in producing goods it can make more efficiently than other countries and trade for goods that others produce better."

For example:

- If England is better at producing textiles and France is better at producing wine, it makes sense for England to focus on textiles and France on wine, then trade.

- If England imposes tariffs on French wine, its consumers would pay higher prices and lose access to the best available product.

Smith believed that removing tariffs would lead to greater prosperity for all nations by allowing them to focus on what they do best.

2.2.2 David Ricardo and Comparative Advantage

Building on Smith's work, David Ricardo introduced the concept of comparative advantage in the early 19th century.

Comparative advantage states that:

- Even if one country is better at producing everything, it should still specialize in the industries where it has the greatest efficiency relative to others.

- Trade allows countries to maximize efficiency and total global production.

Example:

- The U.S. is highly productive in both agriculture and technology.

- However, its advantage in technology is much greater than in agriculture.

- If the U.S. focuses on tech and imports some agricultural goods, the economy as a whole benefits.

Ricardo's theory became the foundation for modern free trade agreements, arguing that tariffs distort economic efficiency and lead to lost potential growth.

2.3 The Protectionist Argument: When Tariffs Are Justified

While free trade has been the dominant economic theory, protectionists argue that tariffs are sometimes necessary for economic and national security reasons.

2.3.1 The Infant Industry Argument (Friedrich List)

Friedrich List, a 19th-century German economist, criticized free trade theory, arguing that young industries in developing nations need protection to grow.

His Infant Industry Argument states that:

- If a country wants to build a new industry (e.g., steel, electronics, semiconductors), it cannot compete immediately with established foreign companies
  .
- Tariffs give domestic companies time to grow, become competitive, and eventually compete globally.

- Once the industry is strong enough, tariffs can be removed.

Example: The U.S. and Steel in the 19th Century

- In the 1800s, the U.S. imposed high tariffs on British steel.

- This helped American steel companies grow without being crushed by British competition.

- Once U.S. steel became strong, tariffs were no longer necessary.

2.3.2 The National Security Argument

Some industries are too important to be left vulnerable to foreign dependence. These include:

- Defense industries (military equipment, aerospace)

- Energy resources (oil, rare earth minerals)

- Food production (agriculture)

Governments may impose tariffs to ensure domestic production remains viable, even if it is not the most economically efficient choice.

Example: The U.S. and Semiconductor Tariffs

- In 2022, the U.S. imposed restrictions on semiconductor exports to China.

- This was not just about economics—it was a security issue.

- The government wanted to ensure the U.S. maintained its technological edge.

2.3.3 The Anti-Dumping Argument

Dumping occurs when a foreign company sells products below cost to drive competitors out of business and gain market control.

- Once competitors are eliminated, the foreign company raises prices and dominates the market.

- Tariffs can prevent dumping and protect domestic industries.

Example: China and Solar Panels

- The U.S. accused China of dumping solar panels at below-market prices, driving American companies out of business.

- In response, the U.S. imposed tariffs to protect its domestic solar industry.

2.3.4 The Job Protection Argument

Tariffs can prevent job losses in industries threatened by cheap imports.

Example: The U.S. and Steel Workers

- U.S. steel companies have struggled against low-cost foreign competition.

- Tariffs on steel imports help keep American steel plants running and protect jobs.

However, critics argue that protecting some jobs through tariffs often destroys jobs in other industries that rely on imports.

2.4 The Modern Debate: Do Tariffs Work?

Economists remain divided on whether tariffs are effective.

Arguments Against Tariffs

- **Higher consumer prices** – Tariffs increase costs for consumers.

- **Trade wars** – Retaliatory tariffs from other countries can hurt exports.

- **Market inefficiencies** – Protectionism can lead to weak, uncompetitive industries.

Arguments in Favor of Tariffs

- **Protecting strategic industries** – Some industries need protection to survive.

- **Job security** – Tariffs prevent outsourcing and offshoring.

- **National security** – Certain industries must remain domestically controlled.

What History Shows

- Tariffs helped the U.S. grow in the 19th century but also contributed to economic crises.

- The Smoot-Hawley Tariff (1930) worsened the Great Depression.

- Modern tariffs on China (2018-2020) had mixed results—some industries benefited, others suffered.

Conclusion

The debate over tariffs is complex, with valid arguments on both sides. While classical economic theory favors free trade, real-world conditions sometimes justify protectionist policies.

Understanding when and where tariffs have worked (or failed) is essential for shaping smart trade policy. In the next chapter, we will examine historical examples of tariffs, including their successes and failures, to see how theory translates into reality.

Chapter 3: The Pros of Tariffs

Tariffs have long been used as a tool for shaping economies, protecting industries, and influencing trade relationships. While many economists argue in favor of free trade, tariffs can offer significant benefits under the right conditions. This chapter explores the advantages of tariffs, analyzing how they protect domestic industries, generate government revenue, encourage local manufacturing, and strengthen national security. By understanding these benefits, we can better evaluate when and how tariffs should be applied to maximize economic growth and stability.

3.1 Protecting Domestic Industries and Jobs

One of the most common arguments in favor of tariffs is that they shield domestic industries from foreign competition. By making imported goods more expensive, tariffs encourage consumers to buy locally produced products, helping domestic companies grow and protecting jobs.

3.1.1 Preventing Outsourcing and Job Losses

Many American industries, particularly in manufacturing, have suffered from outsourcing—the process of moving production to countries where labor is cheaper. Tariffs level the playing field by making foreign goods more expensive, allowing domestic businesses to compete more fairly.

- **Example:** The U.S. Steel Industry

    o In the 1980s and 1990s, cheap steel imports from China and other countries undercut American steel producers.

    o Many U.S. steel mills closed, leading to mass layoffs and economic decline in steel-producing regions.

- In 2018, the U.S. imposed tariffs on steel and aluminum imports, aiming to revive domestic steel production and save jobs.

3.1.2 Supporting Small and Emerging Businesses

Large multinational corporations can often survive global competition, but small and medium-sized businesses struggle to compete with cheap imports. Tariffs protect these businesses by giving them a chance to establish themselves before facing foreign competition.

- **Example:** The U.S. Solar Panel Industry

    - In 2018, the U.S. imposed tariffs on imported solar panels, primarily from China.

    - The goal was to support American solar panel manufacturers that were struggling to compete with low-cost Chinese alternatives.

Without tariffs, many of these smaller companies would fail, leading to job losses and an increased reliance on foreign imports.

3.2 Encouraging Domestic Manufacturing and Economic Growth

Tariffs incentivize businesses to manufacture goods locally rather than relying on foreign imports. By increasing the cost of imported materials and products, tariffs encourage companies to invest in domestic production, creating jobs and boosting the local economy.

3.2.1 Strengthening Industrial Growth

Countries that rely too heavily on imports can become vulnerable to global supply chain disruptions. Encouraging domestic manufacturing ensures that essential industries remain operational, even in times of crisis.

- **Example:** The COVID-19 Pandemic and Medical Supplies

    o Before COVID-19, the U.S. relied heavily on imported medical supplies, particularly from China.

    o When the pandemic hit, global supply chains collapsed, and the U.S. faced severe shortages of masks, ventilators, and pharmaceuticals.

    o Many policymakers argued that tariffs on medical imports could encourage domestic production, reducing dependence on foreign suppliers in future crises.

3.2.2 Attracting Foreign Investment

Tariffs can also make foreign companies invest in domestic production to avoid paying import taxes.

- **Example**: The Auto Industry in the U.S.

    o The U.S. has imposed tariffs on imported automobiles in the past.

    o In response, foreign automakers like Toyota, Honda, and BMW built factories in the U.S., creating thousands of jobs and boosting local economies.

By making it more expensive to import goods, tariffs encourage businesses to establish manufacturing operations within the country, leading to more investment, jobs, and industrial development.

3.3 Generating Government Revenue

Historically, tariffs have been a major source of government income. Before the introduction of income taxes, many governments relied on tariffs to fund infrastructure, military spending, and public services. Even today, tariffs can provide significant revenue for countries that need additional financial resources.

3.3.1 Tariffs as a Source of Public Funding

When tariffs are imposed, foreign exporters pay taxes on their goods before they enter the domestic market. This money goes directly to the government, which can use it for:

- Infrastructure projects (roads, bridges, airports)
- Education and public services
- National defense and military spending
- **Example**: Tariffs in the Early United States

    o In the 1800s, before income tax existed, the U.S. government relied heavily on tariffs for revenue.

    o Tariffs funded the expansion of railroads, the military, and government programs.

    o Even today, tariffs contribute billions of dollars to the federal budget.

3.3.2 Reducing Trade Deficits

A trade deficit occurs when a country imports more than it exports. High trade deficits can lead to:

- Increased borrowing from foreign nations
- Weakened domestic industries
- Currency devaluation

Tariffs can help reduce trade deficits by discouraging imports and encouraging domestic production, improving a country's overall economic balance.

- **Example:** The U.S. and China Trade War (2018-2020)

- The U.S. had a massive trade deficit with China, importing far more than it exported.

- The Trump administration imposed tariffs on hundreds of billions of dollars worth of Chinese goods to reduce the trade imbalance.

While controversial, tariffs can be an effective tool for balancing trade relationships and ensuring a country does not become overly dependent on foreign goods.

3.4 Strengthening National Security and Reducing Foreign Dependence

In some industries, tariffs are not just about economic policy—they are about national security. If a country relies too heavily on foreign goods, it becomes vulnerable to supply chain disruptions, trade wars, and geopolitical conflicts.

3.4.1 Protecting Critical Industries

Certain industries are essential for national security, including:

- Defense manufacturing (weapons, aircraft, military vehicles)
- Energy production (oil, rare earth minerals, nuclear power)
- Food and agriculture

Governments impose tariffs on these industries to ensure they remain domestically controlled and not at the mercy of foreign suppliers.

- **Example:** The U.S. and Rare Earth Minerals

    o Rare earth minerals are critical for making electronics, military equipment, and renewable energy technology.

    o China controls more than 80% of the world's rare earth supply, creating a potential security risk.

    o The U.S. has imposed tariffs and restrictions on rare earth imports, encouraging domestic mining and production.

3.4.2 Preventing Foreign Dependence

If a country becomes too reliant on imports, it risks economic instability if global supply chains break down. Tariffs reduce dependency on foreign countries, ensuring a stable and self-sufficient economy.

- **Example:** Energy Independence

    o Many countries impose tariffs on imported oil to encourage domestic energy production and reduce reliance on foreign suppliers.

    o This protects them from geopolitical conflicts that could disrupt supply chains.

Conclusion

Tariffs, when used correctly, can provide significant economic and strategic benefits. They:

- ✓ Protect domestic industries and jobs
- ✓ Encourage local manufacturing and investment
- ✓ Generate government revenue
- ✓ Reduce trade deficits
- ✓ Strengthen national security

However, tariffs also have downsides, which we will explore in Chapter 4: The Cons of Tariffs. While tariffs can protect industries, they can also lead to higher consumer prices, trade wars, and economic inefficiencies. The key question is whether the benefits outweigh the costs in any given situation.

Chapter 4: The Cons of Tariffs

While tariffs can offer protection to domestic industries, encourage local manufacturing, and strengthen national security, they also come with significant downsides. Tariffs can lead to higher consumer prices, inefficiencies in domestic industries, economic retaliation, and strained international relations.

In this chapter, we will explore the negative effects of tariffs, analyzing real-world examples of how tariffs have harmed economies, disrupted global trade, and led to unintended consequences.

4.1 Higher Prices for Consumers

One of the most immediate and noticeable effects of tariffs is higher prices for consumers. Since tariffs act as a tax on imports, businesses pass the increased costs onto consumers, leading to inflation and reduced purchasing power.

4.1.1 How Tariffs Raise Consumer Costs

When tariffs increase the price of imported goods, businesses often have two choices:

1. Absorb the cost themselves (which reduces profits).
2. Pass the cost onto consumers by increasing prices.

In most cases, businesses raise prices, meaning that ordinary consumers end up paying more for everyday products.

- **Example:** The U.S.-China Trade War (2018-2020)

    o The U.S. imposed tariffs on Chinese electronics, furniture, and household goods.

- o In response, companies like Apple, Walmart, and Target raised prices on their products.

- o As a result, American consumers paid billions of dollars more for goods that were previously cheaper.

4.1.2 Tariffs as a Hidden Tax on Consumers

Although tariffs are technically paid by importers, the burden often falls on consumers. Studies show that higher prices due to tariffs disproportionately affect middle- and lower-income households, who spend a larger percentage of their income on essential goods.

- **Example:** U.S. Tariffs on Washing Machines (2018)

  - o The Trump administration imposed tariffs on imported washing machines to help domestic manufacturers like Whirlpool.

  - o However, the tariffs increased the average price of washing machines by $86 per unit, costing U.S. consumers an estimated $1.5 billion in higher prices.

This demonstrates how tariffs, while aimed at protecting industries, often hurt consumers by making everyday goods more expensive.

4.2 Trade Wars and Retaliation

When one country imposes tariffs, trading partners often retaliate with their own tariffs, leading to trade wars that hurt both sides.

4.2.1 The Domino Effect of Retaliatory Tariffs

- If the U.S. imposes tariffs on Chinese goods, China responds with tariffs on American goods.

- This makes it harder for American businesses to sell products abroad, reducing exports and hurting domestic industries.

- **Example**: The U.S.-China Trade War (2018-2020)

  - The U.S. imposed tariffs on Chinese steel, electronics, and consumer goods.

  - China retaliated with tariffs on American soybeans, pork, and automobiles.

  - As a result, American farmers and automakers suffered billions in lost sales.

4.2.2 The Impact on Farmers and Exporters

Industries that rely on exports often suffer the most from trade wars. When foreign countries impose retaliatory tariffs, American farmers, manufacturers, and exporters lose access to international markets.

- **Example:** U.S. Farmers and Chinese Retaliation

  - In response to U.S. tariffs, China stopped buying American soybeans.

  - Soybean farmers in states like Iowa and Illinois lost billions of dollars in sales.

  - The U.S. government had to bail out farmers with emergency subsidies, costing taxpayers even more money.

This shows how tariffs, which are meant to protect domestic industries, often end up harming other sectors of the economy.

4.3 Market Inefficiencies and Reduced Global Competitiveness

Tariffs shield domestic industries from competition, but this can lead to inefficiencies, lower-quality products, and reduced innovation.

4.3.1 Protecting Inefficient Industries

When industries are protected from competition, they have less incentive to innovate or improve efficiency. Instead of focusing on quality and competitiveness, they rely on government protection.

- **Example:** The U.S. Steel Industry (1970s-1980s)

    - The U.S. imposed tariffs on foreign steel to protect domestic producers.

    - While tariffs helped American steel companies in the short term, they also removed the pressure to innovate.

    - As a result, U.S. steel fell behind technologically, while foreign producers like Japan and Germany became more competitive.

4.3.2 Tariffs Can Lead to Lower Quality Products

When foreign competition is limited, domestic companies may not feel the need to improve their products. This can result in higher prices for lower-quality goods, ultimately hurting consumers.

- **Example:** The U.S. Auto Industry in the 1970s

    - The U.S. imposed tariffs on Japanese cars to protect American automakers.

    - Without competition, U.S. car manufacturers became complacent, producing lower-quality vehicles.

- o Meanwhile, Japanese automakers (Toyota, Honda) continued innovating and improving efficiency, leading to their dominance in the global market.

This demonstrates how tariffs can sometimes hinder rather than help domestic industries by removing the pressure to compete and innovate.

4.4 The Risk of Corruption and Political Influence

When governments impose tariffs, they pick winners and losers in the economy. This often leads to lobbying, corruption, and political favoritism.

4.4.1 Corporations Lobby for Special Protections

Large corporations often lobby for tariffs to protect their industries, even if they are not economically necessary.

- **Example:** The Sugar Industry in the U.S.
    - o The U.S. has imposed high tariffs on foreign sugar for decades.
    - o This benefits a small group of sugar producers but raises prices for consumers and food manufacturers.
    - o The sugar industry spends millions lobbying Congress to keep tariffs in place, even though they hurt the broader economy.

4.4.2 Political Motivations Behind Tariffs

Tariffs are sometimes imposed not for economic reasons, but for political gain.

29

- **Example:** Steel Tariffs and Swing States

    o Many U.S. steel-producing states (like Pennsylvania and Ohio) are key battleground states in elections.

    o Politicians often impose tariffs on steel before elections to win votes, even if the economic benefits are questionable.

This shows how tariffs can be used as a political tool, rather than a carefully planned economic policy.

Conclusion

While tariffs can protect jobs, encourage domestic manufacturing, and improve national security, they also come with major drawbacks:

✘ Higher prices for consumers

✘ Trade wars and economic retaliation

✘ Inefficiencies and reduced global competitiveness

✘ Encouragement of lobbying and corruption

The challenge for policymakers is finding a balance—using tariffs strategically while minimizing their negative effects.

In the next chapter, we will explore historical case studies of tariffs, examining when they worked and when they failed to better understand their real-world impact.

Chapter 5: Tariffs In Early U.S. History (1789–1930)

Tariffs have played a significant role in shaping the economic and political landscape of the United States. From the country's founding through the early 20th century, tariffs were used to fund the government, protect domestic industries, and encourage economic growth. However, they also contributed to sectional tensions, economic downturns, and international conflicts.

This chapter examines the early history of tariffs in the U.S., from Alexander Hamilton's protectionist policies to the high tariffs of the 19th century, leading up to the infamous Smoot-Hawley Tariff Act of 1930, which many historians blame for worsening the Great Depression.

5.1 The Role of Tariffs in Early America (1789–1830)

In the early years of the United States, tariffs were one of the primary sources of government revenue. Since the federal government had no income tax, it relied heavily on tariffs to fund operations, including infrastructure projects, military spending, and public services.

5.1.1 Alexander Hamilton and the Case for Protectionism

One of the earliest advocates for tariffs and protectionism was Alexander Hamilton, the first U.S. Secretary of the Treasury. In his famous Report on Manufactures (1791), Hamilton argued that the young United States needed to:

✅ Protect its emerging industries from British competition

✅ Use tariffs to encourage domestic production

✅ Fund the federal government

Hamilton saw Britain's dominance in manufacturing as a threat to the U.S. economy. At the time, American businesses struggled to compete with British imports, which were cheaper and more advanced due to Britain's industrial revolution.

To solve this, Hamilton proposed protective tariffs to make imported goods more expensive, encouraging Americans to buy domestically made products.

◆ **Outcome:**

- In 1789, the first major U.S. tariff law was passed, imposing import duties of 5%–15% on foreign goods.

- The revenue helped pay off debts from the Revolutionary War.

- While tariffs benefited manufacturers in the North, they hurt Southern farmers, who relied on imported goods.

5.1.2 The Tariff of 1816: America's First Major Protective Tariff

After the War of 1812, American leaders realized that the U.S. was too dependent on British goods. During the war, British trade blockades had crippled the American economy. In response, Congress passed the Tariff of 1816, which:

✓ Imposed a 20-25% tax on imported goods

✓ Was designed to help U.S. industries compete with Britain

✓ Marked the beginning of America's protectionist policies

◆ Outcome:

- Northern manufacturers supported the tariff because it protected their industries.

- Southern states opposed it, fearing higher costs for imported goods.

- This marked the beginning of a long North-South divide over tariffs, which would grow in the coming decades.

5.2 The Tariff of Abominations (1828) and Sectional Conflict

By the 1820s, tariffs had become one of the most divisive issues in American politics.

5.2.1 The Tariff of Abominations (1828)

In 1828, Congress passed a steep tariff on imported goods, raising rates to nearly 40%. This was intended to protect Northern industries but was disastrous for the South, which relied on trade.

◈ Why the South Hated It:

- Southern farmers depended on imported goods from Europe.

- European countries retaliated with their own tariffs, hurting Southern exports (especially cotton).

- Many in the South saw this as favoring Northern industry at their expense.

5.2.2 The Nullification Crisis (1832–1833)

The Tariff of 1828 sparked a constitutional crisis. South Carolina declared the tariff unconstitutional and refused to enforce it.

- President Andrew Jackson threatened military action against South Carolina.

- Eventually, a compromise was reached, lowering tariffs.

- However, the crisis deepened tensions between the North and South, foreshadowing future conflicts leading to the Civil War.

5.3 The Gilded Age and the Rise of High Tariffs (1860–1900)

During the late 19th century, the U.S. pursued some of the highest tariffs in its history.

5.3.1 The Morrill Tariff (1861)

Passed during the early days of the Civil War, this tariff:

☑ Raised duties on imports to protect American industry
☑ Helped fund the Union's war effort
☑ Further alienated the South, which was already preparing to secede

◆ Outcome:

- The high tariffs helped Northern industries grow rapidly.

- The South, now part of the Confederacy, continued to oppose tariffs.

5.3.2 Tariffs and Industrial Expansion

Between 1865 and 1900, the U.S. economy boomed, becoming one of the world's leading industrial powers. High tariffs played a key role in:

- ✓ Protecting American steel, textiles, and manufacturing
- ✓ Encouraging railroad expansion and industrial innovation
- ✓ Increasing federal government revenue

◆ Downside:

- Farmers and consumers often paid higher prices due to reduced competition.

- Other countries retaliated with their own tariffs, making it harder for U.S. farmers to export crops.

5.4 The Smoot-Hawley Tariff (1930) – A Policy Disaster

By the early 20th century, the global economy was becoming more interconnected. However, the Great Depression (1929–1939) led to a resurgence of protectionist policies.

5.4.1 The Smoot-Hawley Tariff Act

In 1930, Congress passed the Smoot-Hawley Tariff Act, which imposed some of the highest tariffs in U.S. history. The goal was to:

- ✓ Protect American jobs and industries
- ✓ Encourage domestic spending

◆ **Outcome:**

- Over 20,000 imported goods were hit with new tariffs.

- Other nations retaliated with their own tariffs, leading to a global trade war.

- U.S. exports dropped by nearly 60%, making the Great Depression even worse.

- Many economists believe the Smoot-Hawley Tariff deepened the economic crisis rather than solving it.

5.5 Key Lessons from Early U.S. Tariff History

Tariffs can support industrial growth – The U.S. became a major manufacturing power in part due to tariffs protecting its industries.

Tariffs create winners and losers – While they help manufacturers, they often hurt farmers and consumers by raising prices.

Retaliation is a serious risk – High tariffs can lead to trade wars, damaging exports.

Political divisions over tariffs can be severe – The North and South had drastically different views on tariffs, contributing to sectional conflicts.

Overuse of tariffs can backfire – The Smoot-Hawley Tariff worsened the Great Depression, showing that extreme protectionism can be harmful.

Conclusion

The early history of U.S. tariffs reveals a complex and often contradictory economic strategy. Tariffs helped build American industry but also created economic and political tensions.

In the next chapter, we will examine the post-World War II shift toward free trade, exploring how the U.S. moved away from tariffs and embraced globalization.

Conclusion

Chapter 6: The Great Depression and The Smoot-Hawley Tariff (1930)

The Smoot-Hawley Tariff Act of 1930 is often cited as one of the most disastrous economic policies in U.S. history. Passed in response to the Great Depression, the tariff was intended to protect American industries and workers. Instead, it triggered a global trade war, deepened the economic crisis, and contributed to a severe decline in international commerce.

In this chapter, we will explore the events leading up to the Smoot-Hawley Tariff, its impact on the U.S. and global economies, and the lessons learned from this failed experiment in protectionism.

6.1 The Economic Crisis of the Great Depression

The Great Depression (1929–1939) was the worst economic downturn in modern history, characterized by:

- **Stock market crash (October 1929)** – Billions of dollars in wealth vanished overnight.

- **Mass unemployment – By 1933**, U.S. unemployment had soared to 25%.

- **Bank failures** – Thousands of banks collapsed, wiping out savings.

- **Deflation and falling demand** – Prices plummeted, making it harder for businesses to stay afloat.

As the economy spiraled downward, politicians sought ways to protect American jobs and industries. One of the most popular ideas was raising tariffs to limit foreign competition and boost domestic production.

6.2 The Smoot-Hawley Tariff Act: Origins and Goals

6.2.1 The Push for Higher Tariffs

- In 1928, Republican President Herbert Hoover ran on a platform of protecting American farmers.

- At the time, farmers were suffering from low crop prices due to overproduction and competition from foreign imports.

- Hoover and Congress believed that higher tariffs would shield American farmers from global competition.

6.2.2 The Passage of the Tariff

- Senator Reed Smoot (R-Utah) and Representative Willis Hawley (R-Oregon) led the push for new tariff legislation.

- The bill originally focused on agriculture but was expanded to include over 20,000 products, from textiles to industrial machinery.

- Despite warnings from economists and business leaders, the bill passed in June 1930, raising tariffs to their highest levels in U.S. history.

◆ **Key Features of the Smoot-Hawley Tariff:**

   ✓ Increased tariffs on over 20,000 imported goods.

   ✓ Raised average tariffs from 38.5% to 60% on dutiable imports.

   ✓ Aimed to protect U.S. farmers and manufacturers from foreign competition.

6.3 The Immediate Effects of the Smoot-Hawley Tariff

6.3.1 Retaliation from Other Countries

As soon as the U.S. enacted the Smoot-Hawley Tariff, other countries retaliated by imposing tariffs on American exports.

- **Canada:** Imposed tariffs on U.S. agricultural products, hurting American farmers.

- **European nations:** Placed duties on American goods, reducing exports of automobiles, machinery, and industrial goods.

- **Latin America:** Shifted trade to Britain instead of buying from U.S. suppliers.

◆ **Result:**

- U.S. exports fell by 61% between 1929 and 1933.

- American farmers, who were supposed to benefit from the tariff, suffered even more because they lost access to foreign markets.

6.3.2 A Collapse in International Trade

Global trade plummeted as countries imposed retaliatory tariffs.

- Total world trade declined by over 65% from 1929 to 1934.

- The League of Nations warned that Smoot-Hawley had worsened the depression worldwide.

- Major industries—like steel, automotive, and manufacturing—suffered as exports dried up.

6.3.3 Rising Unemployment and Economic Decline

Instead of protecting jobs, Smoot-Hawley accelerated job losses.

- Many export-dependent businesses closed, leading to layoffs.

- Unemployment in the U.S. surged from 8% in 1930 to 25% in 1933.

- Even industries that benefited from the tariff initially (like steel and textiles) suffered when other countries cut off trade.

◆ Key Irony:

- The tariff was intended to help farmers, but farm incomes dropped by 50% between 1929 and 1932 due to retaliatory tariffs.

6.4 Political and Economic Backlash

6.4.1 Opposition from Economists and Business Leaders

The Smoot-Hawley Tariff was widely opposed by economists and business leaders. Over 1,000 economists signed a petition urging Hoover to veto the bill—but he signed it anyway.

◆ Warnings from Experts:

- Economist Irving Fisher predicted that the tariff would deepen the economic crisis—and he was right.

- Henry Ford called the bill "an economic stupidity" and personally lobbied against it.

- Wall Street investors feared it would damage global confidence in the U.S. economy—and the stock market continued to decline after its passage.

6.4.2 The Failure of Protectionism

By 1934, it was clear that Smoot-Hawley had backfired. The new Roosevelt administration sought to undo the damage through:

✓ The Reciprocal Trade Agreements Act (1934) – Gave the president power to negotiate lower tariffs with other nations.

✓ A gradual move toward free trade – The U.S. abandoned high tariffs and embraced multilateral trade agreements.

✓ The General Agreement on Tariffs and Trade (GATT) (1947) – This post-WWII agreement helped rebuild global trade.

6.5 Key Lessons from the Smoot-Hawley Tariff

Tariffs Can Worsen Economic Crises

- Instead of protecting jobs, the tariff increased unemployment by reducing trade.

Retaliatory Tariffs Hurt Exporters

- American farmers and manufacturers lost foreign markets, causing bankruptcies.

Global Trade Wars Can Have Lasting Damage

- The collapse in international trade delayed economic recovery for years.

Overprotectionism Can Backfire

- While tariffs help some industries, they often hurt the broader economy.

Conclusion

The End of High Tariffs in the U.S.

The Smoot-Hawley Tariff is considered one of the greatest economic policy mistakes in U.S. history. It turned a deep recession into a full-scale global depression, proving that excessive protectionism can do more harm than good.

In the aftermath of the Great Depression, the U.S. shifted away from high tariffs, moving toward free trade agreements and globalization.

In the next chapter, we will explore how World War II and the post-war era reshaped U.S. trade policy, leading to lower tariffs and the rise of global trade institutions like the World Trade Organization (WTO).

Chapter 7: Post-World War II Trade Liberalization

The aftermath of World War II marked a dramatic shift in global economic policy. The United States, having learned from the mistakes of the Smoot-Hawley Tariff (1930) and the economic devastation of the Great Depression, reversed course on high tariffs and became a leading advocate for free trade.

This chapter explores how the U.S. transitioned from a protectionist trade policy to one centered around trade liberalization, leading to the creation of institutions like the General Agreement on Tariffs and Trade (GATT) and the World Trade Organization (WTO). We will also examine how these changes impacted the U.S. economy, global trade, and industrial development.

7.1 The Economic and Political Landscape After World War II

By 1945, the world had been devastated by World War II. Many countries faced:

- Widespread economic collapse
- Severe shortages of goods and materials
- A need to rebuild industries and economies

Unlike after World War I, where protectionism and trade barriers were widely adopted, world leaders in 1945 recognized that global cooperation and trade were essential for economic recovery.

7.1.1 U.S. Economic Strength and the Need for Trade

Unlike most nations, the U.S. emerged from WWII as an economic superpower:

- ✓ It accounted for 50% of global industrial output in 1945.
- ✓ It had a strong manufacturing base and growing middle class.
- ✓ It needed global markets to sell its surplus goods.

The U.S. recognized that if it wanted to sustain its economic boom, it needed stable trading partners—which meant helping other countries rebuild their economies through trade.

7.1.2 The Failure of Protectionism and the Shift to Free Trade

The devastating effects of the Smoot-Hawley Tariff (1930) had convinced policymakers that high tariffs hurt global economic stability. Many economists and political leaders believed that trade barriers had contributed to the Great Depression and even fueled the rise of extremism leading to WWII.

◆ Lesson Learned:

- Instead of isolating economies through tariffs, the U.S. sought to rebuild the global economy through free trade

- This marked the beginning of a new era: trade liberalization and international economic cooperation.

7.2 The General Agreement on Tariffs and Trade (GATT) (1947)

One of the most significant post-war trade agreements was the General Agreement on Tariffs and Trade (GATT), which was established in 1947.

7.2.1 Goals of GATT

GATT aimed to:

- ✓ Reduce tariffs and trade barriers
- ✓ Encourage free trade among nations
- ✓ Prevent the rise of protectionism

7.2.2 How GATT Worked

- Member countries agreed to gradually lower tariffs through negotiation rounds.

- It introduced the Most-Favored Nation (MFN) principle, meaning that any tariff reduction for one country applied to all GATT members.

- Over time, tariffs on industrial goods dropped significantly, allowing for the growth of global trade.

⬧ Impact on the U.S.:

✓ U.S. exports surged as global markets opened up.

✓ The American economy boomed as manufacturers sold goods worldwide.

✓ Tariff reductions helped create international supply chains.

7.3 The Marshall Plan (1948) and Economic Recovery

Recognizing the need for a strong global economy, the U.S. launched the Marshall Plan (1948), which provided:

$13 billion in aid to rebuild Europe's economies.

Promoted trade liberalization by requiring European nations to reduce tariffs and trade barriers.

◆ Impact:

✅ European economies recovered quickly, leading to increased demand for U.S. goods.

✅ Strengthened U.S.-European trade relations.

✅ Laid the foundation for Western economic cooperation and growth.

7.4 The Shift from Tariffs to Trade Agreements (1950s–1970s)

As GATT reduced tariffs, the U.S. focused on trade agreements to open markets even further.

7.4.1 The Kennedy Round (1964–1967)

- Named after President John F. Kennedy, this was the largest round of GATT negotiations at the time.

- Tariffs on industrial products were cut by 35-50%, expanding global trade.

- The U.S. economy benefited from increased access to European and Asian markets.

7.4.2 The Tokyo Round (1973–1979)

- Addressed non-tariff barriers, such as subsidies and regulations that limited trade.

- Marked the beginning of modern globalization.

◆ Impact on U.S. Industry:

  ✓ U.S. manufacturing and technology sectors expanded into global markets.

  ✓ American companies grew internationally, increasing profits.

  ✓ However, foreign competition also increased, leading to new challenges.

7.5 The Creation of the World Trade Organization (WTO) (1995)

By the 1990s, global trade had outgrown GATT, leading to the creation of the World Trade Organization (WTO) in 1995.

7.5.1 Goals of the WTO

  ✓ Enforce trade agreements between nations.
  ✓ Resolve trade disputes through binding arbitration.
  ✓ Promote global economic stability by ensuring fair trade rules.

♦ U.S. Benefits from the WTO:

✅ Expanded access to global markets for American goods and services.

✅ Stronger intellectual property protections, helping U.S. tech firms.

✅ Helped prevent trade wars by providing a legal framework for resolving disputes.

7.6 The Shift to Free Trade Agreements (1990s–2000s)

Beyond GATT and the WTO, the U.S. pursued regional free trade agreements.

7.6.1 North American Free Trade Agreement (NAFTA) (1994)

- Signed between the U.S., Canada, and Mexico
- Eliminated most tariffs between the three nations.
- Created integrated supply chains, allowing U.S. companies to expand production.

♦ Impact of NAFTA:

✅ U.S. exports to Canada and Mexico skyrocketed.

✅ Helped U.S. industries become more competitive globally.

❌ Some U.S. manufacturing jobs moved to Mexico, leading to job losses in certain industries.

7.6.2 China's Entry into the WTO (2001)

- China joined the WTO in 2001, leading to an explosion in U.S.-China trade.

- Many U.S. industries benefited, but domestic manufacturing jobs declined as companies offshored production.

7.7 The Benefits and Challenges of Trade Liberalization

◆ **Benefits:**

✓ Opened markets for American businesses, increasing exports.

✓ Lowered prices for consumers, increasing purchasing power.

✓ Strengthened global economic cooperation, reducing the risk of trade wars.

◆ **Challenges:**

✗ Some industries suffered job losses due to foreign competition.

✗ China's rise as a global manufacturer led to offshoring of jobs.

✗ Trade imbalances grew, leading to political backlash against free trade.

Conclusion

A New Era of Trade Policy

The post-WWII shift toward trade liberalization transformed the global economy, leading to:

    ✓ A surge in U.S. exports and economic growth.

    ✓ The creation of institutions like the WTO to regulate trade.

    ✓ Global supply chains that increased efficiency but created new challenges.

In the next chapter, we will explore modern trade disputes, including the rise of China, the renegotiation of NAFTA into the United States-Mexico-Canada Agreement (USMCA), and the Trump-era tariffs on steel, aluminum, and Chinese goods.

Chapter 8: Modern Tariffs – Nafta, China, And the Trump Era

The 21st century has seen significant shifts in U.S. trade policy, marked by globalization, free trade agreements, and rising tensions with China. After decades of promoting trade liberalization, the U.S. has increasingly turned back to tariffs in response to economic and political challenges.

This chapter explores the evolution of U.S. trade policy in recent decades, focusing on NAFTA, China's rise as a manufacturing powerhouse, and the Trump administration's aggressive use of tariffs. We will analyze the effects of these policies and their implications for the future of U.S. trade.

8.1 NAFTA: The North American Free Trade Agreement (1994–2020)

The North American Free Trade Agreement (NAFTA) was one of the most controversial trade deals in U.S. history. Signed in 1994 by the U.S., Canada, and Mexico, it aimed to eliminate tariffs and trade barriers between the three countries.

8.1.1 Goals of NAFTA

✓ Promote economic integration between the U.S., Canada, and Mexico.

✓ Eliminate tariffs on most goods traded between the three nations.

✓ Strengthen North American supply chains.

✓ Increase foreign investment in all three countries.

8.1.2 The Economic Impact of NAFTA

◆ Positive Effects:

✓ **Increased trade** – U.S. trade with Canada and Mexico more than tripled from $290 billion in 1993 to over $1.1 trillion by 2016.

✓ **Lower prices** – Consumers benefited from cheaper goods, especially in industries like automobiles and agriculture.

✓ **Boosted U.S. agricultural exports** – American farmers gained easier access to Canadian and Mexican markets.

◆ Negative Effects:

✗ **Manufacturing job losses** – Many U.S. factories moved production to Mexico to take advantage of lower wages.

✗ **Trade deficits** – The U.S. trade deficit with Mexico grew, leading to political backlash.

✗ **Uneven benefits** – While corporations and consumers benefited, some U.S. workers and communities suffered.

8.1.3 Trump's Renegotiation: The USMCA (2020)

In response to criticism that NAFTA harmed American workers, President Donald Trump renegotiated the deal into the United States-Mexico-Canada Agreement (USMCA), which:

✓ Increased labor protections in Mexico to reduce the incentive for outsourcing.

✓ Required that 75% of a car's parts must be made in North America (up from 62.5%) to qualify for tariff-free trade.

✓ Allowed stronger enforcement of trade rules.

◆ Outcome:

- Some economists argue the changes were minor and NAFTA's basic framework remained intact.

- However, USMCA gained bipartisan support and was seen as an improvement over NAFTA.

8.2 The Rise of China and U.S. Trade Imbalances

While NAFTA was a key issue in North America, China's entry into the World Trade Organization (WTO) in 2001 had an even bigger impact on U.S. trade policy.

8.2.1 China's Entry into the WTO (2001)

In 2001, China joined the WTO, gaining access to global markets with lower tariffs. Many U.S. policymakers believed:

✓ Trade with China would benefit both countries.

✓ China would move toward a more market-driven economy.

✓ American consumers would benefit from cheaper goods.

8.2.2 The U.S.-China Trade Deficit

However, U.S. imports from China skyrocketed, while exports to China did not grow as fast.

- The U.S. trade deficit with China grew from $83 billion in 2001 to $375 billion in 2017.

- Millions of U.S. manufacturing jobs disappeared as companies offshored production to China.

- China subsidized its industries and allegedly engaged in unfair trade practices (such as currency manipulation and intellectual property theft).

8.2.3 China's Manufacturing Dominance

◆ Why Did U.S. Companies Move to China?

    ✓ **Lower labor costs** – Wages in China were significantly lower than in the U.S.

    ✓ **Government incentives** – China provided subsidies and tax breaks to attract foreign companies.

    ✓ **Massive supply chains** – China developed highly efficient manufacturing hubs, especially in electronics and textiles.

◆ **Consequences for the U.S.:**

    ✗ **U.S. factory closures** – Cities like Detroit and Pittsburgh suffered as manufacturing jobs moved overseas.

    ✗ **Trade dependency on China** – The U.S. became heavily reliant on Chinese imports for electronics, pharmaceuticals, and consumer goods.

    ✗ **Political backlash** – Both Democrats and Republicans criticized China's trade practices, leading to calls for tariffs.

8.3 The Trump Administration's Use of Tariffs (2017–2020)

In response to rising trade deficits and job losses, President Donald Trump implemented aggressive tariffs as part of his "America First" trade policy.

8.3.1 The Steel and Aluminum Tariffs (2018)

- Trump imposed 25% tariffs on steel and 10% tariffs on aluminum imports.

- The goal was to revive American metal industries and protect national security.

⬧ **Results:**

✓ Short-term boost for U.S. steel companies.

✗ Higher costs for manufacturers (automakers and construction firms paid more for materials).

✗ Retaliation from allies – Canada, the EU, and China imposed counter-tariffs on U.S. products.

8.3.2 The U.S.-China Trade War (2018–2020)

Trump escalated trade tensions by imposing tariffs on $250 billion worth of Chinese goods, including:

✓ Electronics
✓ Machinery
✓ Textiles

⬧ **China retaliated with tariffs on American soybeans, pork, and cars.**

Results:

✅ Some U.S. manufacturers moved production out of China (to Vietnam, India, and Mexico).

❌ U.S. farmers suffered billions in losses as China cut soybean purchases.

❌ Prices for American consumers increased on goods like electronics and appliances.

❌ The trade war caused uncertainty in global markets, affecting stock prices and investment.

8.4 Did Trump's Tariffs Work?

The impact of Trump's tariffs remains debated.

Successes:

✅ Brought attention to unfair Chinese trade practices.
✅ Encouraged companies to reduce reliance on China.
✅ Led to the U.S.-China Phase One Trade Deal (2020), where China agreed to buy more American goods.

Failures:

❌ Did not bring back large-scale manufacturing jobs.
❌ Increased costs for American businesses and consumers.
❌ Did not significantly reduce the trade deficit.

8.5 The Biden Administration's Approach to Tariffs

After Trump left office, President Joe Biden maintained many of the Trump-era tariffs but shifted the focus toward multilateral trade cooperation.

Biden's Trade Policies (2021–2025):

✓ Kept tariffs on China in place but sought more diplomatic solutions.

✓ Worked with allies to counter China's influence rather than acting unilaterally.

✓ Invested in domestic industries (e.g., semiconductor production) rather than relying solely on tariffs.

Summary of Trumps declared Tariffs as of Mar 9th 2025

As of March 9, 2025, President Donald Trump's tariff policies have significantly impacted international trade:

Canada and Mexico:

- **Initial Tariffs:** On February 1, 2025, Trump announced 25% tariffs on all imports from Canada and Mexico, excluding Canadian energy imports, which faced a 10% tariff. These measures aimed to address concerns over illegal immigration and drug trafficking, particularly fentanyl.

- **Temporary Suspension:** Following negotiations, a one-month suspension of these tariffs was agreed upon after Canada and Mexico committed to enhancing border security measures.

- **Implementation:** Despite initial delays, the tariffs were enforced on March 4, 2025, leading to retaliatory measures from both nations. Canada imposed 25% tariffs on $30 billion worth of U.S. goods, with plans to expand this to $125 billion. Mexico's response is anticipated to be announced on March 9, 2025.

China:

- **Escalating Tariffs:** The U.S. increased tariffs on Chinese imports from 10% to 20% on March 4, 2025, intensifying trade tensions.

- **Chinese Retaliation:** In response, China imposed additional tariffs on U.S. agricultural products and initiated investigations into certain U.S. companies.

Global Trade Implications:

- **Steel and Aluminum:** The administration announced 25% tariffs on all steel and aluminum imports, effective March 12, 2025, removing previous exemptions.

- **Economic Impact:** These policies have contributed to stock market volatility and raised concerns about potential inflation and disruptions in global supply chains.

Overall, President Trump's tariff strategies reflect a protectionist approach, aiming to address national security concerns and promote domestic industries, while eliciting significant international responses.

Conclusion

The Future of Tariffs in U.S. Trade Policy

The past two decades have seen a re-evaluation of free trade policies, with tariffs being used as a tool for economic protectionism, national security, and political leverage.

As we move forward, key questions remain:

- Will tariffs help rebuild American manufacturing?

- How will the U.S. manage trade relations with China?

- Can tariffs be used without sparking trade wars?

In the next chapter, we will explore the impact of tariffs on the global supply chain and the future of international trade.

Chapter 9: The Global Supply Chain and Tariffs

The global supply chain has become an essential part of modern economies, connecting industries, businesses, and consumers across multiple countries. However, the increasing use of tariffs as an economic and political tool has disrupted supply chains, causing ripple effects throughout the world.

In this chapter, we will explore how tariffs impact global supply chains, examine real-world examples of tariff-induced disruptions, and analyze the strategies businesses and governments use to navigate these challenges.

9.1 Understanding the Global Supply Chain

A global supply chain is a network of companies, manufacturers, and suppliers that work together to produce and distribute goods across different countries.

◆ **Key Characteristics of Global Supply Chains:**

 ✓ **Interconnected production** – Products are often assembled from parts made in different countries.

 ✓ **Just-in-time manufacturing** – Many businesses keep minimal inventory, relying on fast, efficient supply chains.

 ✓ **Cost-driven production** – Companies manufacture goods in low-cost regions (e.g., China, Vietnam, Mexico).

9.1.1 Why Businesses Depend on Global Supply Chains

Companies rely on global supply chains for several reasons:

✅ **Lower costs** – Businesses reduce expenses by manufacturing in countries with cheaper labor and raw materials.

✅ **Efficiency and specialization** – Different regions specialize in different components (e.g., semiconductors in Taiwan, textiles in Bangladesh).

✅ **Access to new markets** – Companies expand their reach by operating in multiple countries.

However, when tariffs disrupt supply chains, businesses face higher costs, production delays, and supply shortages.

9.2 How Tariffs Disrupt Global Supply Chains

When a country imposes tariffs, it affects the entire supply chain, leading to:

❌ Increased costs for raw materials and components

❌ Production slowdowns due to price hikes and delays

❌ Shifts in manufacturing locations to avoid tariffs

9.2.1 Case Study: The U.S.-China Trade War and Supply Chain Disruptions

The 2018–2020 U.S.-China trade war forced many businesses to rethink their supply chains.

◆ Key Tariffs:

- The U.S. imposed tariffs on Chinese electronics, machinery, and raw materials.

- China retaliated with tariffs on U.S. agricultural products and automobiles.

◆ Impact on Supply Chains:

✗ **Higher costs for U.S. manufacturers** – Companies that relied on Chinese-made parts (e.g., Apple, Ford, Boeing) faced price increases.

✗ **Delays in production** – Supply chain disruptions slowed down factory output.

✗ **Shift to other countries** – Some companies moved production to Vietnam, India, and Mexico to avoid tariffs.

9.2.2 The Semiconductor Shortage and Tariff Effects

- The U.S. imposed export restrictions on semiconductors to China, citing national security concerns.

- China responded with restrictions on rare earth minerals used in electronics.

- This contributed to a global semiconductor shortage, affecting industries like automobiles, consumer electronics, and defense manufacturing.

◆ Result:

- Car prices surged due to a lack of computer chips

- Tech companies struggled to meet demand for smartphones, laptops, and gaming consoles.

9.3 Strategies Businesses Use to Adapt to Tariffs

9.3.1 Relocating Manufacturing to Other Countries

To avoid tariffs, many companies move production away from affected countries.

- **Example**: Apple and Vietnam – In response to U.S. tariffs on China, Apple shifted some iPhone and AirPods production to Vietnam.

- **Example**: Clothing Industry and Bangladesh – Many apparel companies moved from China to Bangladesh to avoid tariffs and reduce labor costs.

9.3.2 Reshoring and Nearshoring: Bringing Manufacturing Closer to Home

Some companies move production back to the U.S. or nearby countries to reduce reliance on overseas supply chains.

- **Example:** The U.S. Auto Industry – Some American automakers, including Ford and GM, have expanded production in the U.S. and Mexico.

- **Example:** Semiconductor Manufacturing – The U.S. passed the CHIPS Act (2022) to boost domestic semiconductor production, reducing reliance on Taiwan and China.

9.3.3 Diversifying Suppliers

Companies now source materials from multiple suppliers to reduce the risk of tariff-related disruptions.

- **Example:** Retail and E-Commerce – Companies like Walmart and Amazon now source from multiple countries instead of relying on a single supplier.

9.4 Government Responses to Supply Chain Disruptions

9.4.1 The U.S. CHIPS and Science Act (2022)

- The U.S. government invested $52 billion to boost domestic semiconductor manufacturing.

- This aims to reduce reliance on China and Taiwan for advanced chips.

9.4.2 The Inflation Reduction Act (2022)

- Encourages companies to manufacture electric vehicles, batteries, and clean energy products in the U.S..

- Tariffs on Chinese-made solar panels and batteries are used to promote domestic clean energy production.

9.5 The Future of Global Supply Chains and Tariffs

◆ Will More Companies "Reshore" to the U.S.?

- Some companies are moving manufacturing back to the U.S. due to geopolitical risks.

- However, higher U.S. labor costs make it difficult to reshore all industries.

◆ Will Tariffs Continue to Disrupt Global Trade?

- Many experts believe tariffs will remain a tool for economic and national security policies.

- Governments may use tariffs selectively to protect strategic industries (e.g., defense, energy, technology).

◆ Will New Trade Agreements Reduce Tariff Barriers?

- Regional trade agreements (like USMCA and the Indo-Pacific Economic Framework) may help companies adjust to new trade dynamics.

- The WTO may play a role in reducing tariff conflicts between major economies.

Conclusion

A Changing Trade Landscape

Tariffs have fundamentally changed global supply chains, forcing businesses and governments to adapt to a new economic reality.

◆ Key Takeaways:

✓ Tariffs raise costs and disrupt supply chains, forcing companies to rethink sourcing strategies.

✓ Businesses are diversifying suppliers and shifting production to avoid reliance on any single country.

✓ Governments are using industrial policies to encourage domestic manufacturing.

As we move forward, the question remains: Will tariffs continue to shape global trade, or will new policies create a more stable supply chain?

In the next chapter, we will explore who wins and who loses under tariff policies, analyzing their impact on businesses, workers, and consumers.

Chapter 10: Winners And Losers of Tariff Policies

Tariffs are often promoted as a tool to protect domestic industries, create jobs, and reduce trade imbalances. However, they also come with significant economic consequences that do not affect all groups equally. While some industries and workers benefit from tariffs, others suffer higher costs, reduced market access, or job losses.

In this chapter, we will explore who wins and who loses when tariffs are imposed, analyzing their effects on businesses, workers, consumers, and the global economy.

10.1 Winners: Who Benefits from Tariffs?

10.1.1 Domestic Industries Protected from Foreign Competition

The biggest winners of tariff policies are domestic industries that compete with imported goods. When tariffs are imposed, foreign products become more expensive, making domestically produced goods more attractive.

◆ **Example:** The U.S. Steel Industry

- In 2018, President Donald Trump imposed 25% tariffs on steel imports to protect U.S. steel manufacturers.

- As a result, American steel companies saw increased demand and higher profits.

- U.S. Steel announced a $750 million investment to expand operations, creating new jobs.

✦ Other Industries That Benefit from Tariffs:

✓ Textiles and apparel – Tariffs on foreign clothing help U.S. manufacturers compete.

✓ Automobile manufacturing – Protecting domestic car makers from cheaper imports.

✓ Technology and semiconductors – Recent tariffs on Chinese microchips have encouraged domestic chip production.

10.1.2 Workers in Protected Industries

Tariffs help preserve jobs in industries that face outsourcing and foreign competition.

✦ **Example:** U.S. Aluminum Workers (2018 Tariffs)

- In response to 10% aluminum tariffs, companies reopened aluminum plants.

- Thousands of jobs were saved in Kentucky, Missouri, and other states.

However, the long-term impact on jobs is debatable, as tariffs can lead to higher costs for other industries that rely on these materials.

10.1.3 Governments That Collect Tariff Revenue

When tariffs are imposed, the government collects billions of dollars in additional tax revenue from importers.

◆ Example: U.S. Tariff Revenue (2018-2020)

- The Trump administration's tariffs on China generated over $80 billion in additional revenue.

- This revenue can be used for infrastructure, subsidies, or economic relief programs.

However, tariffs are often a hidden tax on consumers, as importers pass higher costs on to buyers.

10.1.4 Countries with Domestic Substitutes for Imported Goods

If a country produces alternatives to imported goods, tariffs can encourage consumers to buy local products.

◆ Example: India's Agricultural Tariffs

- India imposed high tariffs on imported wheat and rice to protect local farmers.

- As a result, Indian farmers saw higher prices for their crops and greater demand.

However, if domestic industries cannot fully meet demand, tariffs can cause shortages and inflation.

10.2 Losers: Who Suffers from Tariffs?

10.2.1 Consumers Paying Higher Prices

One of the biggest downsides of tariffs is that they raise prices for consumers. When businesses pay higher costs for imported goods, they often pass these costs onto customers.

◆ **Example:** U.S. Washing Machine Tariffs (2018)

- In 2018, the U.S. imposed tariffs on imported washing machines to help domestic manufacturers.

- As a result, the average price of a washing machine rose by $86 per unit.

- American consumers paid an estimated $1.5 billion in higher prices.

◆ **Industries with Higher Prices Due to Tariffs:**

✗ Electronics – Tariffs on Chinese goods increased prices for laptops and smartphones.

✗ Automobiles – Tariffs on steel raised the cost of cars.

✗ Food and agriculture – Tariffs on foreign goods led to higher grocery prices.

10.2.2 Exporters Facing Retaliation from Other Countries

When a country imposes tariffs, trading partners often respond with their own tariffs, hurting exporters.

◆ **Example:** U.S. Farmers and China's Retaliation (2018 Trade War)

- The U.S. imposed tariffs on Chinese steel and electronics.

- China retaliated by imposing tariffs on U.S. soybeans and pork.

- As a result, U.S. farmers lost billions in sales, leading to government bailouts.

Industries Hurt by Retaliatory Tariffs:

✖ Agriculture – Soybean, pork, and dairy exports fell.

✖ Manufacturing – U.S. carmakers lost access to Chinese and European markets.

✖ Technology – Tariffs on U.S. software and hardware increased costs for global tech companies.

10.2.3 Companies That Rely on Imported Materials

Many U.S. manufacturers depend on imported raw materials (e.g., steel, aluminum, semiconductors). When tariffs raise costs, companies face higher production expenses.

Example: U.S. Auto Industry and Steel Tariffs (2018)

- The 25% tariff on imported steel increased costs for U.S. automakers.

- Ford and GM reported higher expenses, leading to price hikes on vehicles.

Other Affected Industries:

✖ Construction – Higher costs for steel and aluminum raised housing prices.

✖ Electronics – Tariffs on Chinese components hurt U.S. tech firms.

✖ Renewable energy – Solar panel tariffs increased costs for clean energy projects.

10.2.4 Retailers and Small Businesses

Large companies like Walmart, Amazon, and Home Depot rely on cheap imports to keep prices low. When tariffs increase costs, they must:

- Raise prices on clothing, furniture, and electronics.

- Absorb losses, reducing profits and investments.

- Shift suppliers to avoid tariffs, disrupting operations.

◆ **Example: Small Businesses and China Tariffs (2019)**

- Many small businesses relied on cheap Chinese imports for resale.

- Trump's tariffs on Chinese goods increased their costs, forcing them to raise prices or cut jobs.

10.2.5 Countries Dependent on Trade

Countries that rely on exports suffer when tariffs limit market access.

◆ **Example:** The European Union's Retaliation Against U.S. Tariffs (2018)

- After the U.S. imposed steel tariffs, the EU responded with tariffs on American whiskey, motorcycles, and jeans

- This hurt U.S. companies like Harley-Davidson, which saw a decline in European sales.

◆ Other Countries Affected by U.S. Tariffs:

✖ Mexico and Canada – Faced tariffs on steel and aluminum before the USMCA agreement.

✖ Germany and Japan – Faced threats of auto tariffs.

✖ China – Lost access to U.S. markets for key exports.

10.3 Balancing the Pros and Cons of Tariffs

While tariffs can protect domestic industries, they also hurt consumers, exporters, and businesses.

◆ When Tariffs Are Beneficial:

✓ Protecting critical industries (e.g., defense, energy, semiconductors)

✓ Preventing unfair trade practices (e.g., dumping, currency manipulation).

✓ Encouraging domestic investment and reducing reliance on foreign goods.

◆ When Tariffs Are Harmful:

✖ When they increase costs for consumers without long-term benefits.

✖ When they provoke trade wars that hurt exporters and farmers.

✖ When they reduce business competitiveness by raising material costs.

Conclusion

The Complexity of Tariff Policies

Tariffs create both winners and losers, making them one of the most complex tools in economic policy. While they can protect domestic industries and jobs, they also risk higher costs, trade conflicts, and economic inefficiencies.

In the next chapter, we will explore how tariffs influence inflation and whether they make economic conditions worse.

Chapter 11: Tariffs And Inflation – Are They Making Things Worse?

Tariffs are often used to protect domestic industries and jobs, but they can also contribute to inflation, increasing the cost of goods and services for businesses and consumers. As global supply chains become more interconnected, the impact of tariffs on prices has grown more significant than ever.

In this chapter, we will explore how tariffs affect inflation, analyze historical and modern examples, and assess whether tariffs are making economic conditions worse in today's world.

11.1 Understanding Inflation and Its Causes

11.1.1 What Is Inflation?

Inflation is the rise in prices of goods and services over time, which reduces the purchasing power of money.

⬧ **Common Causes of Inflation:**

✓ Increased production costs – Higher costs for raw materials, labor, and transportation.

✓ Demand-pull inflation – When demand for goods exceeds supply, leading to higher prices.

✓ Monetary policy – When central banks print too much money, causing currency devaluation.

✓ Supply chain disruptions – When global events (e.g., COVID-19, war, tariffs) limit the availability of goods.

11.2 How Tariffs Contribute to Inflation

When a government imposes tariffs, it raises the cost of imported goods. This forces businesses to increase prices, leading to inflation.

⬥ **Key Ways Tariffs Contribute to Inflation:**

✖ Higher raw material costs – Tariffs on steel, aluminum, and semiconductors raise costs for manufacturers.

✖ Increased consumer prices – Tariffs on foreign products force retailers to charge more.

✖ Supply chain disruptions – When tariffs disrupt trade, shortages cause price spikes.

11.2.1 The Supply Chain Effect

- If the U.S. imposes tariffs on Chinese-made electronics, companies like Apple and Dell must pay more for components.
- These higher costs get passed on to consumers, increasing inflation.

⬥ **Example: U.S. Steel and Aluminum Tariffs (2018)**

- The 25% tariff on steel and 10% tariff on aluminum raised costs for:
    - Car manufacturers (Ford, GM)
    - Construction companies
    - Household appliance makers

- This led to higher prices for cars, homes, and consumer goods.

11.3 Historical Case Studies: Tariffs and Inflation

11.3.1 The Smoot-Hawley Tariff and the Great Depression (1930s)

- The Smoot-Hawley Tariff Act (1930) imposed high tariffs on over 20,000 imported goods

- This triggered global retaliation, leading to:
  - A collapse in international trade.
  - Higher prices for essential goods.
  - A deepening of the Great Depression.

- Prices for goods rose due to supply shortages, worsening the economic crisis.

11.3.2 The 1970s Oil Crisis and Trade Barriers

- In the 1970s, tariffs on foreign oil and OPEC's production cuts led to:
  - Oil price spikes (gasoline prices quadrupled).
  - Rising costs for transportation and manufacturing.
  - Overall inflation hitting 14% in the U.S..

◆ **Lesson: Tariffs on essential goods (oil, steel) worsen inflation, making everyday products more expensive.**

11.4 The Modern Impact of Tariffs on Inflation

11.4.1 The U.S.-China Trade War (2018–2020)

The U.S.-China trade war led to higher prices for businesses and consumers.

◆ Key Tariffs and Their Impact:

- Tariffs on Chinese electronics and machinery → Higher prices for computers, smartphones, and appliances.

- Tariffs on steel and aluminum → More expensive cars, washing machines, and homes.

- Chinese retaliatory tariffs on U.S. agriculture → Higher food costs for American consumers.

◆ Inflationary Impact:

✘ U.S. inflation rose by an estimated 0.5%–1.0% due to tariffs.

✘ A study found that American consumers paid an additional $52 billion in higher costs.

✘ Retailers like Walmart and Target raised prices on imported goods.

11.4.2 COVID-19, Supply Chains, and Tariff Effects

During COVID-19, global supply chains were already strained, and tariffs made things worse:

- Tariffs on Chinese medical supplies led to higher costs for masks, gloves, and ventilators.

- Tariffs on semiconductors contributed to chip shortages, increasing prices for cars and electronics.

- Shipping delays and port congestion further increased inflation.

◆ Lesson:

Tariffs exacerbated inflationary pressures by making essential goods more expensive during a crisis.

11.5 Do Tariffs Always Cause Inflation?

While tariffs often lead to higher prices, there are some exceptions:

◆ When Tariffs May Not Cause Inflation:

✓ If domestic producers can meet demand – If tariffs encourage local production, price increases may be minimal.

✓ If the currency strengthens – A stronger U.S. dollar can offset tariff-related cost increases.

✓ If tariffs target luxury goods – Tariffs on high-end products (e.g., luxury cars, designer clothing) may not impact overall inflation.

◆ Example: Japan's Protectionist Policies (1960s-1980s)

- Japan used tariffs to protect its domestic auto and electronics industries.

- However, because Japanese companies were highly competitive, tariffs did not lead to major inflation.

11.6 Alternatives to Tariffs for Controlling Trade and Inflation

If tariffs contribute to inflation, what alternative policies can be used?

◆ Alternative Strategies:

✓ Trade agreements – Bilateral and multilateral trade deals reduce dependency on one country.

✓ Domestic investment – Encouraging local manufacturing can reduce reliance on imports.

✅ Subsidies instead of tariffs – Providing tax breaks or incentives for domestic industries can achieve similar protection without raising prices.

◆ **Example: The CHIPS Act (2022)**

- Instead of tariffs, the U.S. invested $52 billion in domestic semiconductor production.

- This aims to reduce dependency on China while avoiding inflationary pressure.

11.7 The Future: Will Tariffs Continue to Drive Inflation?

11.7.1 The Biden Administration's Approach

President Joe Biden kept many Trump-era tariffs but introduced more targeted policies:

✅ Strategic tariffs – Maintaining tariffs on China for national security reasons.

✅ Lowering tariffs on consumer goods – Reducing costs for middle-class families.

✅ Investing in supply chain resilience – Expanding domestic manufacturing to reduce reliance on imports.

11.7.2 Will Tariffs Be Used Differently in the Future?

◆ **Key Trends to Watch:**

- Governments may use tariffs selectively to avoid inflationary effects.

- The U.S. may shift focus from broad tariffs to targeted industrial policies.

- Digital and service-based economies may reduce dependence on physical imports, lessening the need for tariffs.

Conclusion

Are Tariffs Making Things Worse?

◆ **YES, tariffs contribute to inflation when:**

✗ They increase costs for raw materials and consumer goods.

✗ They disrupt global supply chains.

✗ They lead to retaliatory trade wars, worsening economic conditions.

◆ **NO, tariffs may not worsen inflation when:**

✓ They encourage domestic production without supply shortages.

✓ They target non-essential goods or luxury items.

✓ They are offset by strong monetary policy and economic stability.

In the next chapter, we will explore the political debate around tariffs, examining how different political parties and ideologies view tariffs and their impact on trade and the economy.

Chapter 12: The Politics of Tariffs – Left Vs. Right Perspectives

Tariffs have long been a divisive political issue, shaping debates about trade, economic policy, and national security. While both conservatives and progressives have used tariffs throughout history, their reasons for supporting or opposing them have evolved.

This chapter explores how different political ideologies—conservatives, progressives, libertarians, and centrists—view tariffs, and how shifting economic realities have influenced their positions.

12.1 The Conservative Argument for Protectionism

Historically, Republicans and conservatives have had a complex relationship with tariffs. While early conservatives supported free trade, modern conservatives—especially in the Trump era—have embraced economic nationalism and protectionism.

12.1.1 Why Many Conservatives Support Tariffs Today

⬥ **Protecting American Jobs**

- Conservatives argue that free trade agreements and outsourcing have hurt American workers.

- Tariffs, they say, prevent companies from offshoring jobs to lower-wage countries like China and Mexico.

⬥ **National Security and Economic Independence**

- Many conservatives view China as an economic and geopolitical threat.

- Tariffs on semiconductors, rare earth minerals, and tech products are seen as essential for reducing dependence on foreign nations.

◆ Revitalizing Manufacturing and Blue-Collar Industries

- Tariffs are promoted as a way to rebuild America's industrial base.

- **Example:** Trump's steel and aluminum tariffs (2018) aimed to revive U.S. metal production.

12.1.2 The Trump Era and Republican Support for Tariffs

◆ Trump's "America First" Trade Policy

- 25% tariffs on steel and 10% on aluminum

- Tariffs on $250 billion in Chinese goods

- Renegotiation of NAFTA into the USMCA

◆ Republican Shift Toward Protectionism

- Historically, Republicans favored free trade (e.g., Reagan and Bush supported globalization).

- Trump's trade war with China marked a major shift toward economic nationalism.

◆ Conservative Critics of Tariffs

- Pro-business Republicans (e.g., Mitch McConnell, Paul Ryan) opposed tariffs, arguing they hurt small businesses and raise prices.

- Many farmers and exporters in red states suffered from retaliatory tariffs (e.g., China stopped buying U.S. soybeans).

◆ Post-Trump Era: Will Conservatives Keep Supporting Tariffs?

- Some Republicans want to continue tariffs to counter China.

- Others want a return to free trade to boost economic growth.

12.2 The Progressive Argument for Tariffs

While progressives often advocate for worker protections and environmental regulations, their stance on tariffs is more complicated.

12.2.1 Why Some Progressives Support Tariffs

◆ Protecting American Workers from Exploitation

- Progressives argue that unregulated free trade allows corporations to exploit cheap labor in countries with poor working conditions.

- Tariffs can pressure foreign companies to improve wages and labor standards.

◆ Fighting Climate Change and Environmental Harm

- Many low-cost manufacturing nations have weaker environmental protections.

- Green tariffs (taxes on imports from polluting countries) could reduce global emissions.

◆ Fair Trade Instead of Free Trade

- Progressives support trade policies that prioritize workers over corporate profits.

- **Example:** The USMCA included stronger labor protections for Mexican workers, pushed by progressive Democrats.

12.2.2 Why Some Progressives Oppose Tariffs

◆ **Higher Prices for Consumers**

- Tariffs often increase the cost of essential goods, which hurts low-income families the most.

◆ **Risk of Trade Wars Hurting U.S. Farmers and Small Businesses**

- Many progressive-leaning regions, especially in the Midwest and agricultural states, suffered from China's retaliatory tariffs.

◆ **Alternative Policies to Tariffs**

- Progressives favor domestic investments (e.g., infrastructure, job training, subsidies for green energy) over tariffs as a tool for economic growth.

12.3 The Libertarian and Free-Market Perspective

◆ **Libertarians strongly oppose tariffs, viewing them as:**

    ✕ Government interference in the free market
    ✕ A hidden tax on consumers
    ✕ A cause of economic inefficiency

12.3.1 The Case for Free Trade

✓ Free trade allows countries to specialize, improving efficiency.

✓ Consumers benefit from lower prices and greater choice.

✓ Trade wars disrupt economic growth and lead to retaliatory measures.

⬥ **Famous Libertarian Critics of Tariffs:**

- Milton Friedman – Argued that free trade benefits all nations.
- Ron Paul – Criticized tariffs as a form of "economic warfare."

⬥ **Example: U.S. Tariffs on Solar Panels (2018)**

- The Trump administration imposed tariffs on Chinese solar panels to protect U.S. producers.

- Libertarians opposed the move, arguing it raised costs for clean energy projects.

12.4 Centrists and the Balanced Approach

◆ **Centrists believe in a mix of free trade and strategic protectionism.**

12.4.1 When Tariffs Are Justified

✓ To protect national security (e.g., semiconductors, defense industries).

✓ To respond to unfair trade practices (e.g., China's state-subsidized industries).

✓ To reduce dependency on authoritarian regimes.

12.4.2 When Free Trade Is Preferable

✅ For consumer goods and technology (keeping prices low).

✅ For industries that benefit from global cooperation (e.g., medical supplies, agriculture).

◆ Example: The Biden Administration's Approach to Tariffs

- Kept many Trump-era tariffs on China, arguing they are necessary for economic security.

- Reduced tariffs on certain consumer goods to ease inflation pressures.

- Increased domestic investment (e.g., CHIPS Act for semiconductor manufacturing) instead of relying solely on tariffs.

12.5 The Future of Tariff Politics

◆ Will Republicans Continue to Support Tariffs?

- Some conservatives want permanent tariffs on China and Mexico

- Others believe tariffs hurt U.S. businesses and raise costs.

◆ Will Progressives Push for "Green Tariffs"?

- The Biden administration has explored tariffs on imports from high-emission countries to fight climate change.

◆ Will Free-Market Advocates Regain Influence?

- If inflation remains high, calls for lowering tariffs to reduce costs may gain support.

◆ Will a Balanced Approach Prevail?

- Future trade policy will likely mix tariffs for strategic industries with free trade for consumer goods.

Conclusion

The Political Divide on Tariffs

◆ **Conservatives (Trump Era Republicans):**

   ✅ Support tariffs to protect American jobs and industries.

◆ **Progressives:**

   ✅ Support tariffs for labor rights and environmental policies.

◆ **Libertarians:**

   ✗ Oppose tariffs as government interference in free trade.

◆ **Centrists (Biden's Approach):**

   ~ Use tariffs selectively while promoting global trade.

Tariffs will remain a key political issue, influencing debates on jobs, trade, national security, and inflation.

In the next chapter, we will explore historical examples of when tariffs have succeeded and failed, analyzing key lessons for the future.

Chapter 13: When Do Tariffs Work?

Tariffs have been used for centuries, but their effectiveness depends on economic conditions, policy implementation, and global trade dynamics. While some tariffs have successfully protected industries and fostered economic growth, others have led to higher consumer prices, retaliation, and economic stagnation.

This chapter explores historical and modern examples of tariffs that worked, analyzing the conditions that contributed to their success.

13.1 Key Conditions for Tariffs to Succeed

Tariffs are most effective when:

✓ They support a strategic industry that can become globally competitive.

✓ Domestic alternatives exist, preventing shortages and inflation.

✓ They are temporary, allowing industries time to grow.

✓ They do not provoke damaging retaliation from trading partners.

✓ They target unfair trade practices (e.g., dumping, subsidies).

13.2 Successful Tariffs in U.S. History

13.2.1 The Tariff of 1816: America's First Protective Tariff

Objective:

- Protect American industries from cheap British imports after the War of 1812.

Policy:

- Imposed a 20-25% tariff on manufactured goods, particularly textiles and iron products.

Results:

✅ Encouraged industrialization – Helped U.S. textile mills and ironworks compete with Britain.

✅ Reduced reliance on foreign goods, strengthening the American economy.

✅ Created jobs in northern manufacturing hubs.

◆ Why It Worked:

- The U.S. was already developing its industries, so tariffs gave them a competitive edge without causing major shortages.

- Britain's post-war flooding of the U.S. market with cheap goods threatened domestic growth, making protectionism necessary.

13.2.2 The Morrill Tariff (1861): Funding the Civil War and Industrial Growth

Objective:

- Raise government revenue for the Union war effort
- Protect U.S. manufacturers from European competition.

Policy:

- Increased tariffs on iron, steel, and manufactured goods from 19% to nearly 50%.

Results:

✓ Provided essential funding for the Union Army.

✓ Helped U.S. industries grow rapidly during and after the war.

✓ Boosted railroad expansion and steel production.

⬧ Why It Worked:

- The U.S. was undergoing an industrial revolution, and tariffs accelerated domestic production.
- Post-war, the U.S. became one of the world's leading industrial powers.

13.2.3 The Rise of Japan's Auto Industry (1950s-1980s)

Objective:

- Protect Japan's automotive industry from foreign competition.

Policy:

- High tariffs and import restrictions on foreign cars.
- Government subsidies to support domestic automakers.

Results:

✓ Helped Toyota, Honda, and Nissan become global leaders.

✓ Created millions of high-paying jobs in Japan.

✓ Allowed Japan to develop cutting-edge auto technology.

◆ **Why It Worked:**

- Tariffs were temporary – once Japanese automakers became competitive, restrictions were gradually reduced.

- Government support ensured that domestic companies improved quality and efficiency.

13.2.4 The U.S. Semiconductor Tariffs and the CHIPS Act (2022-Present)

Objective:

- Reduce U.S. dependence on Chinese and Taiwanese semiconductor production.

Policy:

- Tariffs and export restrictions on Chinese microchips

- $52 billion investment in domestic semiconductor manufacturing.

Results (Early Indicators):

✓ Intel and TSMC investing in new chip plants in the U.S..

✓ Reduced reliance on foreign semiconductor production.

✓ Encouraging long-term national security and economic stability.

◆ Why It Might Work:

- Semiconductors are a strategic industry, critical for national security and technological leadership.

- Government investment complements tariffs, ensuring a stable domestic supply.

13.3 Lessons from Successful Tariffs

◆ Tariffs work best when they are part of a broader strategy that includes

✓ Investment in domestic production (e.g., Japan's auto industry, U.S. semiconductors).

✓ Temporary protection that allows industries time to grow.

✓ Avoiding excessive retaliation to prevent economic downturns.

In the next chapter, we will examine historical examples where tariffs failed, analyzing the consequences of poor tariff policies.

Chapter 14: When Do Tariffs Fail?

While tariffs can protect industries and create jobs under the right conditions, history has shown that they can also backfire, leading to economic downturns, trade wars, and higher costs for consumers. In many cases, tariffs have been implemented without a long-term strategy, resulting in unintended consequences.

This chapter explores historical and modern examples where tariffs failed, analyzing the economic and political reasons behind their failures.

14.1 Key Reasons Why Tariffs Fail

✦ **Tariffs often fail when:**

> ✘ They cause price increases that hurt consumers and businesses.

> ✘ They trigger trade wars that damage exports and economic growth.

> ✘ They protect inefficient industries that do not improve over time.

> ✘ They are applied without a clear long-term strategy.

> ✘ They lead to retaliation from other countries, harming global trade.

14.2 Historical Examples of Tariff Failures

14.2.1 The Smoot-Hawley Tariff (1930) – A Global Trade Disaster

Objective:

- Protect U.S. farmers and manufacturers from foreign competition during the Great Depression.

Policy:

- Imposed the highest tariffs in U.S. history, raising duties on over 20,000 imported goods.

What Went Wrong?

✗ Retaliation from other countries – Over 40 nations imposed tariffs on U.S. goods.

✗ Collapse of international trade – Global trade fell by 65% between 1929 and 1934.

✗ Worsened the Great Depression – Unemployment in the U.S. soared from 8% to 25%.

✗ Hurt American farmers – U.S. agricultural exports dropped as foreign markets shut down.

◆ **Key Lesson:**

- Tariffs should not be used as an economic recovery tool during a financial crisis.

- Trade wars harm both importers and exporters, making everyone worse off.

14.2.2 The Chicken Tax (1964) – Unintended Consequences for the U.S. Auto Industry

Objective:

- Retaliate against European tariffs on U.S. poultry.

Policy:

- The U.S. imposed a 25% tariff on imported light trucks from Europe.

What Went Wrong?

✖ Limited consumer choice – Foreign automakers stopped importing small trucks to the U.S. market.

✖ Hurt U.S. manufacturers – While it protected domestic truck makers, it also stifled innovation and competition.

✖ Long-term industry distortion – The tariff remained in place for decades, leading to higher truck prices for American consumers.

◆ Key Lesson:

- Retaliatory tariffs can have long-term negative effects on domestic markets.

- Protecting one industry at the expense of innovation and competition can be harmful.

14.2.3 The U.S.-China Trade War (2018-2020) – Higher Costs, Limited Benefits

Objective:

- Reduce the U.S. trade deficit with China and pressure China to change its trade practices.

Policy:

- Imposed tariffs on $250 billion worth of Chinese goods, including electronics, machinery, and textiles.

- China retaliated with tariffs on U.S. soybeans, pork, and cars.

What Went Wrong?

✖ Higher prices for consumers – American businesses and families paid over $52 billion in additional costs due to tariffs.

✖ Hurt U.S. farmers – China stopped buying American soybeans, forcing the U.S. to bail out farmers with subsidies.

✖ Limited success in reshoring jobs – Despite tariffs, many companies did not bring manufacturing back to the U.S., instead shifting production to Vietnam and Mexico.

✖ Trade deficit barely changed – The U.S. trade deficit with China remained high, despite tariffs.

◆ Key Lesson:

- Tariffs alone do not force companies to bring jobs back - other policies (like subsidies and domestic investment) are needed.

- Retaliation can hurt the industries tariffs are supposed to protect.

14.2.4 The Argentina Soybean Tariffs (2002-2015) – Self-Inflicted Economic Damage

Objective:

- Encourage domestic soybean processing and protect Argentine manufacturers.

Policy:

- High export taxes on raw soybeans, forcing farmers to sell to domestic processors instead of exporting.

What Went Wrong?

✗ Farmers suffered massive losses as their profits were cut.

✗ Soybean production declined, leading to a loss of global market share.

✗ Black markets emerged as farmers smuggled soybeans to avoid tariffs.

✦ Key Lesson:

- Tariffs on critical exports can harm a country's own industries instead of helping them.

- Overregulation can drive businesses underground, reducing government revenue.

14.3 Why Some Tariffs Fail and Others Succeed

◆ **Factors That Lead to Tariff Failures:**

> ✘ **Lack of domestic alternatives** – If there are no local replacements for imported goods, tariffs simply raise costs.

> ✘ **Excessive retaliation** – Trade wars reduce exports and hurt multiple industries.

> ✘ **Permanent protectionism** – If industries never improve, tariffs create long-term inefficiencies.

> ✘ **Poor economic timing** – Tariffs during recessions can worsen economic downturns.

◆ **Factors That Lead to Tariff Success:**

> ✓ Used for strategic industries (e.g., semiconductors, defense).

> ✓ Accompanied by domestic investment (e.g., infrastructure, job training).

> ✓ Temporary and phased out once industries are competitive.

> ✓ Target unfair trade practices rather than broad sectors.

Conclusion

Avoiding the Pitfalls of Bad Tariff Policy

◆ Key Takeaways:

> ✗ Tariffs fail when they increase consumer prices, provoke retaliation, and do not strengthen domestic industries.

> ✓ Tariffs work best when they are part of a broader economic strategy that includes investment and innovation.

As we move forward, the challenge for policymakers is finding the right balance between free trade and protectionism.

In the next and final chapter, we will explore the future of tariffs in the U.S., offering recommendations on how to use tariffs effectively in today's economy.

Chapter 15: A Balanced Approach – What Should the U.S. Do?

Tariffs remain one of the most controversial economic tools in trade policy. While they can protect industries, create jobs, and strengthen national security, they also increase prices, disrupt supply chains, and provoke retaliation.

The challenge for policymakers is finding the right balance—using tariffs strategically without harming the broader economy. In this chapter, we will explore how the U.S. can develop a smarter tariff strategy, ensuring that trade policies serve both economic and national interests.

15.1 The Key Trade Policy Dilemma: Free Trade vs. Protectionism

Over the past century, the U.S. has shifted between free trade and protectionist policies depending on political and economic conditions.

◈ **When Free Trade Works Best:**

 ✅ Encourages global trade and economic growth.

 ✅ Reduces costs for businesses and consumers.

 ✅ Prevents trade wars and economic retaliation.

◈ **When Protectionism Works Best:**

 ✅ Helps new industries develop (infant industry protection).

 ✅ Shields critical industries from foreign control.

 ✅ Counters unfair trade practices like dumping and subsidies.

◆ **The Reality**:

- A purely free trade system can weaken domestic industries and increase dependence on foreign production.

- A purely protectionist system can raise prices and isolate the economy from global opportunities.

◆ **The Best Solution:**

✓ A balanced approach—using targeted tariffs to protect essential industries while maintaining free trade where it benefits consumers and businesses.

15.2 When the U.S. Should Use Tariffs

The U.S. should use tariffs selectively, ensuring they serve strategic and economic goals rather than being a reactionary policy.

15.2.1 Protecting National Security Industries

Some industries are too important to be controlled by foreign powers. Tariffs can help secure supply chains for:

✓ Semiconductors – The U.S. relies heavily on Taiwan and China for computer chips. Tariffs and domestic investment (like the CHIPS Act) can strengthen U.S. production.

✓ Defense manufacturing – Military technology and defense equipment should not depend on foreign suppliers.

✓ Energy production – Tariffs on imported energy materials can boost domestic oil, gas, and renewable energy production.

◆ Example: U.S. Semiconductor Tariffs and Investment

- Tariffs on Chinese microchips have encouraged companies like Intel and TSMC to build factories in the U.S.

- This reduces dependence on China, improving both economic security and national defense.

15.2.2 Responding to Unfair Trade Practices

When countries manipulate trade through subsidies, dumping, or currency manipulation, tariffs can be an effective countermeasure.

✓ Anti-dumping tariffs – Prevent foreign companies from selling products below cost to drive competitors out of business.

✓ Counter-subsidy tariffs – Stop countries like China from unfairly subsidizing their industries to dominate global markets.

◆ Example: Steel and Aluminum Tariffs (2018)

- The U.S. imposed tariffs on steel and aluminum to counteract Chinese overproduction and artificially low prices.

- This protected American steelworkers, though it also increased costs for U.S. manufacturers.

15.2.3 Reducing Dependence on Geopolitical Rivals

The COVID-19 pandemic and rising U.S.-China tensions have highlighted the risks of relying too much on foreign supply chains.

◆ Key Industries to Reshore with Tariffs & Incentives:

✅ Medical supplies – Reduce dependence on China for pharmaceuticals and protective equipment.

✅ Battery production – Shift electric vehicle (EV) battery supply chains away from China.

✅ Food production – Ensure agricultural independence.

◆ Example: The Inflation Reduction Act (2022)

- Encourages domestic EV battery production instead of relying on China.

- Uses tariffs and tax incentives to bring manufacturing back to the U.S.

15.3 When the U.S. Should Avoid Tariffs

While some tariffs serve strategic purposes, others can do more harm than good.

15.3.1 When Tariffs Increase Consumer Prices

Tariffs on everyday consumer goods can drive up costs for American families.

◆ Better Alternative:

- Use subsidies instead of tariffs—for example, support U.S. manufacturers without raising prices for consumers.

15.3.2 When Tariffs Lead to Trade Wars

Trade wars can hurt U.S. exporters, particularly in agriculture and manufacturing.

◈ Example: U.S.-China Trade War (2018-2020)

> ✘ The U.S. imposed tariffs on $250 billion worth of Chinese goods.

> ✘ China retaliated with tariffs on U.S. soybeans, pork, and automobiles.

> ✘ Farmers lost billions in exports, forcing the government to provide bailouts.

◈ Better Alternative:

- Negotiate trade agreements to address unfair practices without triggering large-scale retaliation.

15.3.3 When Tariffs Protect Inefficient Industries

Some industries fail to improve despite years of tariff protection.

◈ Example: The U.S. Sugar Tariffs

- The U.S. has high tariffs on foreign sugar to protect domestic producers.
- As a result, Americans pay nearly double the global price for sugar.
- Meanwhile, candy manufacturers moved production to Mexico and Canada, reducing U.S. jobs.

- **Better Alternative:**

  - Gradually reduce tariffs while investing in modernizing domestic industries.

15.4 A Smarter Tariff Strategy for the Future

To create a balanced, effective trade policy, the U.S. should:

- Use tariffs selectively for national security and unfair trade practices.

- Avoid broad consumer tariffs that increase inflation.

- Encourage reshoring through a mix of tariffs and tax incentives.

- Negotiate trade deals instead of relying solely on tariffs.

- **Example**: The Biden Administration's Tariff Approach

  ✔ Kept many Trump-era tariffs on China to counter unfair trade.

  ✔ Lowered some consumer goods tariffs to reduce inflation.

  ✔ Increased domestic investment in key industries instead of pure protectionism.

Conclusion: The Future of U.S. Tariffs

Tariffs are a powerful but risky tool. When used strategically, they can protect national security, counter unfair trade practices, and promote domestic industries. However, when misused, they can raise costs, trigger trade wars, and hurt the economy.

◆ The Best Approach Moving Forward:

> ✓ Use tariffs only when necessary (e.g., for national security and strategic industries).

> ✓ Invest in domestic manufacturing so industries can compete globally without long-term protection.

> ✓ Negotiate strong trade agreements to prevent trade wars and maintain access to global markets.

The future of U.S. trade policy will require a smarter, more balanced approach—one that supports American businesses and workers without sacrificing economic growth.

Final Thoughts

This book has explored the history, impact, and future of tariffs, highlighting their benefits, risks, and role in shaping global trade. Whether tariffs help or hurt depends on how, when, and why they are applied.

As the world faces new economic challenges—from supply chain disruptions to geopolitical conflicts—the U.S. must adapt its trade policies to ensure long-term prosperity.

Final Conclusion: The Future Of Tariffs In U.S. Trade Policy

Tariffs have been one of the most powerful and controversial tools in economic history. From protecting American industries to triggering global trade wars, their impact has shaped economies, political landscapes, and international relations for centuries.

As the U.S. faces new economic challenges, including globalization, supply chain disruptions, and geopolitical conflicts, the role of tariffs must be reassessed. Rather than relying on broad, reactionary tariffs, the U.S. should adopt a strategic, balanced approach that considers both short-term economic needs and long-term national interests.

Key Takeaways from This Book

1. Tariffs Can Protect National Security and Critical Industries

✅ When used strategically, tariffs can help industries like semiconductors, defense, and energy grow stronger and reduce reliance on foreign suppliers.

2. Tariffs Can Backfire and Hurt the Economy

✖ Poorly implemented tariffs—like the Smoot-Hawley Tariff (1930) and the U.S.-China trade war tariffs (2018-2020)—can increase prices, provoke retaliation, and hurt exporters.

3. A Mixed Approach is Best

◈ The U.S. should combine targeted tariffs with investment in domestic industries, trade agreements, and strategic partnerships to remain competitive.

The Future of U.S. Tariff Policy

Moving forward, the U.S. should:

♦ Use tariffs selectively, focusing on national security, unfair trade practices, and essential industries.

♦ Avoid tariffs that raise costs for consumers and businesses, especially on everyday goods.

♦ Encourage reshoring through a mix of tariffs, tax incentives, and infrastructure investment.

♦ Work with allies to counter economic threats, instead of imposing unilateral tariffs that spark trade wars.

The global economy is evolving, and U.S. trade policy must evolve with it. By making smart, well-calculated decisions, the U.S. can maintain its economic strength while ensuring a fair and competitive trade environment.

The debate over tariffs will continue, as economic conditions, political priorities, and international relations change. There is no one-size-fits-all solution, but history teaches us that a thoughtful, strategic approach works better than extreme protectionism or unchecked free trade.

The challenge for policymakers is to strike the right balance—protecting American industries and workers without causing unnecessary economic harm. If done wisely, tariffs can remain an effective tool for U.S. economic success in the 21st century.

Thank You for Reading!

This book has explored the history, successes, failures, and future of tariffs. Whether you are a policymaker, economist, business owner, or an informed citizen, understanding tariffs is essential for navigating the global economy.

If you enjoyed this book, consider:

> Exploring more on global trade and economic policy.

> Engaging in discussions about the future of U.S. trade policy.

> Thinking critically about how economic decisions impact everyday life.

The future of trade is still being written. Let's make sure it's one that benefits everyone.

Other books by this Author

Francis Williams

The DeepSeek Revolution: How a New AI Model is Redefining the Future of Technology and Society   ISBN: 978-0-9952409-5-7

Master Your Life: only IF... Rudyard Kipling's Stoic Wisdom for the Manic Modern World   ISBN: 978-0-9952409-1-9

Silver and Gold: Your Insurance Policy Against Monetary Debasement, the Global Debt Crisis, and Financial Collapse ISBN: 978-0-9952409-7-1

Bibliography

This bibliography includes sources on tariffs, trade policy, economic history, and global trade relations that have informed the discussions in this book. It covers historical accounts, academic research, government reports, and expert analyses to provide a well-rounded perspective on the impact of tariffs.

Books and Academic Sources

- Baldwin, Robert E. The Political Economy of U.S. Import Policy. MIT Press, 1985.
- Bhagwati, Jagdish. Protectionism. MIT Press, 1988.
- Douglas A. Irwin. Clashing Over Commerce: A History of U.S. Trade Policy. University of Chicago Press, 2017.
- Eichengreen, Barry. Globalizing Capital: A History of the International Monetary System. Princeton University Press, 2008.
- Frieden, Jeffry A. Global Capitalism: Its Fall and Rise in the Twentieth Century. W.W. Norton & Company, 2006.
- Ha-Joon Chang. Kicking Away the Ladder: Development Strategy in Historical Perspective. Anthem Press, 2002.
- Krugman, Paul. Pop Internationalism. MIT Press, 1997.
- Rodrik, Dani. Straight Talk on Trade: Ideas for a Sane World Economy. Princeton University Press, 2017.
- Stiglitz, Joseph E. Globalization and Its Discontents Revisited: Anti-Globalization in the Era of Trump. W.W. Norton & Company, 2018.

Historical Case Studies and Economic Reports

- U.S. Department of Commerce. Economic Impact of Tariffs on U.S. Industries and Consumers. Government Printing Office, 2019.
- U.S. International Trade Commission (USITC). The Economic Effects of Significant U.S. Import Restraints, 2021.
- Federal Reserve Bank of New York. Trade Policy Uncertainty and the Global Economy, 2020.
- World Trade Organization (WTO). Trade and Tariffs in the 21st Century, 2022.
- General Agreement on Tariffs and Trade (GATT). Historical Analysis of Tariff Reductions, 1985.

Government and Policy Documents

- Smoot-Hawley Tariff Act (1930). U.S. Congress, Public Law No. 71-361.
- North American Free Trade Agreement (NAFTA), 1994. U.S., Canada, Mexico.
- United States-Mexico-Canada Agreement (USMCA), 2020.
- U.S. Trade Representative (USTR). Section 301 Investigation into China's Trade Practices, 2018.
- The CHIPS and Science Act (2022). U.S. Government Legislation.
- Inflation Reduction Act (2022). U.S. Government Legislation.

Articles, Reports, and Online Resources

- Bown, Chad P. "The 2018 Trade War and U.S. Manufacturing." Peterson Institute for International Economics, 2019.
- Frankel, Jeffrey A. "The Death of Global Trade? Tariffs and the Future of U.S. Trade Policy." Harvard Kennedy School, 2020.
- Irwin, Douglas A. "The Truth About Tariffs: What History Tells Us." Foreign Affairs, 2019.
- Krugman, Paul. "What Economists Get Wrong About Trade." The New York Times, 2021.
- Mankiw, N. Gregory. "The Case for Free Trade." Brookings Institution, 2018.
- Stiglitz, Joseph. "Why Protectionism Fails." Project Syndicate, 2017.
- World Economic Forum. "The Future of Global Supply Chains and Trade Policy." WEF Report, 2021.

This bibliography provides a comprehensive foundation for further research on tariffs, trade policy, and their effects on the economy. It includes historical perspectives, economic theories, case studies, and policy recommendations to help readers explore the topic in greater depth.

Glossary

This glossary provides definitions of key terms related to tariffs, trade policy, and global economics, helping readers better understand the concepts discussed throughout this book.

A

Ad Valorem Tariff – A tariff calculated as a percentage of the value of the imported good. Example: A 10% tariff on a $1,000 product results in a $100 tax.

Anti-Dumping Tariff – A tariff imposed to prevent foreign companies from selling products below cost to eliminate competition.

Absolute Advantage – An economic principle where a country can produce a good more efficiently than another country.

Autarky – A situation where a country does not trade with others and is self-sufficient.

B

Balance of Trade – The difference between a country's exports and imports. A trade surplus occurs when exports exceed imports, and a trade deficit occurs when imports exceed exports.

Beggar-Thy-Neighbor Policy – A trade policy, such as tariffs or currency devaluation, that benefits one country at the expense of another.

Bilateral Trade Agreement – A trade agreement between two countries that outlines terms for reducing tariffs and trade barriers.

C

Comparative Advantage – The ability of a country to produce a good at a lower opportunity cost than another country, even if it is not the most efficient producer.

Compound Tariff – A tariff that includes both a fixed fee and an ad valorem component (e.g., $5 per unit + 10% of the product's value).

Countervailing Duties – Tariffs imposed to counteract foreign subsidies that give an unfair advantage to imported goods.

D

Dumping – When a company or country sells goods at a lower price than production costs to eliminate competitors.

Duty-Free – Goods that can be imported without paying tariffs or taxes.

E

Economic Nationalism – A policy emphasizing domestic industry protection through tariffs, subsidies, and restrictions on foreign trade.

Embargo – A government-imposed ban on trade with a specific country or on specific goods.

Export Tariff – A tax placed on goods leaving a country, which is uncommon but sometimes used for strategic commodities.

F

Fair Trade – A trade policy that prioritizes labor rights, environmental protections, and ethical sourcing over pure cost efficiency.

Foreign Direct Investment (FDI) – When a company from one country invests in business operations or assets in another country.

Free Trade Agreement (FTA) – An agreement between countries to reduce or eliminate tariffs and trade barriers (e.g., NAFTA, USMCA).

G

General Agreement on Tariffs and Trade (GATT) – A global trade agreement, signed in 1947, that laid the foundation for reducing tariffs and creating the WTO.

Global Supply Chain – A network of suppliers, manufacturers, and distributors across multiple countries that contribute to the production of goods.

Green Tariffs – Tariffs imposed on imports from countries with weaker environmental regulations to encourage sustainable practices.

H

Harmonized System (HS Code) – An internationally standardized system for classifying traded products and determining tariff rates.

Historical Tariff Protectionism – The use of tariffs in the past to develop domestic industries, such as the U.S. steel and textile industries in the 19th century.

I

Import Quota – A limit on the amount of a specific good that can be imported into a country.

Import Substitution – A strategy where a country reduces reliance on imports by developing domestic industries.

Infant Industry Argument – The idea that new industries need temporary protection from international competition to grow and become competitive.

J

Job Outsourcing – The practice of relocating jobs to foreign countries where labor costs are lower, often influenced by trade policies.

L

Laissez-Faire Trade – A policy of minimal government intervention in trade, favoring free-market competition.

Logistics Tariff Impact – The way tariffs disrupt global supply chains, affecting production and shipping costs.

M

Mercantilism – An early economic theory that promoted trade surpluses and high tariffs to accumulate national wealth.

Most-Favored Nation (MFN) Status – A trade rule where a country must offer the same tariff rates to all trading partners unless part of a special trade deal.

N

Non-Tariff Barriers (NTBs) – Restrictions on trade that aren't tariffs, such as import licenses, quotas, or product safety regulations.

North American Free Trade Agreement (NAFTA) – A 1994 trade agreement between the U.S., Canada, and Mexico, later replaced by USMCA in 2020.

O

Opportunity Cost – The economic cost of choosing one trade policy over another, such as protecting domestic industries vs. accessing cheaper imports.

Outsourcing vs. Reshoring – Outsourcing refers to moving production abroad, while reshoring is bringing production back to the home country.

P

Protectionism – The use of tariffs, quotas, and trade barriers to protect domestic industries from foreign competition.

Preferential Trade Agreement (PTA) – A deal between countries that reduces tariffs for specific goods or industries.

Q

Quota – A restriction on how much of a product can be imported or exported in a given time period.

R

Reciprocal Tariff – A tariff that is imposed in response to another country's tariff.

Retaliatory Tariff – A tariff imposed as punishment for another country's trade actions, often leading to a trade war.

Reshoring – Moving manufacturing or jobs back to the home country to reduce reliance on foreign production.

S

Sanctions – Trade restrictions imposed by a country to punish another nation's policies or actions.

Smoot-Hawley Tariff Act (1930) – A highly protectionist U.S. tariff law that worsened the Great Depression by triggering a global trade war.

Specific Tariff – A fixed fee per unit of an imported good, regardless of its price (e.g., $5 per barrel of oil).

Subsidy – Government financial aid given to domestic industries to help them compete against imports.

T

Tariff – A tax on imported (or sometimes exported) goods, designed to raise revenue or protect domestic industries.

Tariff Escalation – When tariff rates increase as products become more processed, discouraging imports of finished goods.

Trade Balance – The difference between exports and imports in a country's economy.

Trade Deficit – When a country imports more than it exports, often leading to political debates over tariffs and trade policy.

Trade Surplus – When a country exports more than it imports, seen as beneficial by protectionist policymakers.

Trade War – A cycle of retaliatory tariffs between countries, often leading to economic damage for both sides.

U

United States-Mexico-Canada Agreement (USMCA) – The updated version of NAFTA, signed in 2020, which added labor protections, environmental regulations, and new trade rules.

Unilateral Tariff – A tariff imposed by a country without negotiation or agreement with other nations.

V

Value-Added Tariff – A tariff imposed on products at different stages of production, often applied to prevent outsourcing of manufacturing.

W

World Trade Organization (WTO) – A global trade body that regulates international trade, resolves disputes, and promotes lower tariffs.

www.ingramcontent.com/pod-product-compliance
Lightning Source LLC
Chambersburg PA
CBHW060044210326
41520CB00009B/1264